Praise for
PEOPLE DO~~N'T~~ CHANGE

"In today's world, where change is the only constant, the biggest challenge for leaders isn't just managing the unknown—it's inspiring their teams to embrace it. Elisabeth White nails it with a fresh, empowering approach that every leader needs right now."

MEL ROBBINS, bestselling author and host of *The Mel Robbins Podcast*

"Everyone is in favor of progress—it's the changes that we don't like! In *People Do Change*, Elisabeth White provides the game plan to flip that conclusion by building a team that embraces a new attitude: 'Together, we win!'"

LES STECKEL, veteran NFL coach; colonel (retired), US Marine Corps Reserve; former president and CEO, Fellowship of Christian Athletes

"As a leader who believes in the power of people-centered approaches, *People Do Change* resonated deeply with me. Elisabeth White's insight into Human-Centric Change Management aligns perfectly with the type of leadership I advocate—one that places empathy, adaptability, and connection at the forefront. In my experience as CEO of the Branson Centre of Entrepreneurship, I've seen firsthand how supporting and empowering individuals creates lasting, meaningful transformation. This book is a vital resource for leaders who understand that real change happens only when we inspire people to grow alongside our vision. I highly recommend it for those who want to lead with heart and purpose."

LAURI-ANN AINSWORTH, CEO, Branson Centre of Entrepreneurship

"Elisabeth White's *People Do Change* is a groundbreaking exploration of navigating change in today's fast-paced world. When people feel like they are part of the solution rather than just the subject of change, they are more likely to embrace it and work toward its success."

SUZANNE MARTIN, bestselling author of *Brilliant Leadership: Patterns for Creating High-Impact Teams* and director of marketing, Learning & Development, Google

"My main mantra in both life and business is 'People first, always!' So it is an absolute delight to provide a testimonial for this fabulous book that confirms what we all know, though many deny . . . the winds of change are constantly blowing. In a business world overwhelmed with processes and technology, we have forgotten what sits at the heart of every organization—its people. If you want to achieve effective and enduring change, then you need to unleash your people. *People Do Change* will help you do just that."

MARCUS DIMBLEBY, coauthor of *Big Things F@$t*, managing director at Effective Direction, and Royal Air Force wing commander (retired)

www.amplifypublishinggroup.com

People Do Change: How to Turn Reluctance into Confidence Using Human-Centric Change Management

©2025 Elisabeth White. All Rights Reserved. No part of this publication may be reproduced, stored in a retrieval system or transmitted in any form by any means electronic, mechanical, or photocopying, recording or otherwise without the permission of the author.

Some names and identifying details have been changed to protect the privacy of individuals and organizations. The views and opinions expressed in this book are solely those of the author. The author and publisher do not assume and hereby disclaim any liability to any party for any loss, damage, or disruption caused by errors or omissions, whether such errors or omissions result from negligence, accident, or any other cause.

Edited by Susan Gaigher

For more information, please contact:
Amplify Publishing, an imprint of Amplify Publishing Group
620 Herndon Parkway, Suite 220
Herndon, VA 20170
info@amplifypublishing.com

Library of Congress Control Number: 2024925636

CPSIA Code: PRV0125A

ISBN-13: 979-8-89138-519-1

Printed in the United States

Author and dad at Super Bowl XXXII, January 25, 1998, San Diego, California. One of the best days of the author's life—Broncos 31, Packers 24.

To Dad (Papa John . . . not the pizza guy),

You saw the leader in me long before I recognized it in myself. Your unwavering confidence in my abilities, your patient guidance through every challenge, and your willingness to be both mentor and cheerleader have shaped my career. This book wouldn't exist without our countless conversations and your endless belief in me.

Through you, I learned that the most powerful change begins with someone who believes in you completely. You've been that someone for me, Dad. Every day of my life!

Thanks for making "daddy's girl" feel like my most impressive job title.

With love and a lifetime of gratitude,

Beat (Elisabeth . . . not the queen)

ELISABETH WHITE

PEOPLE DO~~N'T~~ CHANGE

HOW TO TURN RELUCTANCE
INTO CONFIDENCE USING
**HUMAN-CENTRIC
CHANGE MANAGEMENT**

CONTENTS

Author's Note....................xi

Preface........................xiii

1. Change Is Hard 1
2. Change Management from 1950 to Now................... 9
3. The Problem(s) to Be Solved 35
4. Transforming Change from Challenge to Opportunity 47
5. A Tale of Two Approaches 57
6. Human-Centric Change Management (Unpacked) 69
7. Integrating Agile and Human-Centric Change Management................... 91

8. Using Kanban to Visualize Change Initiatives............ **105**

9. The Art of Communication........ **115**

10. Reimagining Change Management Roles............. **125**

11. Leading Human-Centric Change Management **135**

12. Taking the First Step............ **153**

13. Conclusion **163**

Bibliography **167**

About the Author **171**

AUTHOR'S NOTE

As we've learned from Vernice "FlyGirl" Armour . . .

"No one likes change but a baby!"

Choosing to change often means challenging the status quo, being fearless through the unknown, or relinquishing control. Change comes with risks. Cheers to the *risk-takers* and the *change-makers*!

Live it, love it, be it, do it!

PREFACE

Change: Simply put, change is to make or become different. It's the process of transforming from one state to another. In your business environment, this could mean anything from adopting innovative technologies to restructuring your organization.

The Winds of Change . . .

Welcome to the world of constant change! As you navigate your organization through today's turbulent corporate reality, you might feel like you're trying to sail a ship through a perpetual storm. Don't worry—you're not alone. In fact, you're in good company with leaders across industries who are grappling with the same challenges.

Remember the days when change was a rare event, carefully planned and meticulously executed? Well, those days are long gone. In today's fast-paced, technology-driven world, change is the only constant. But here's the kicker—while the business world has accelerated, human nature hasn't quite caught up. Your workforce, the heart and soul of your organization, might not be as quick to embrace change as your strategic plans require.

So what's a forward-thinking leader like you to do? How can you keep up with the relentless pace of change while also considering the impact this may have on the people in your organization? That's exactly what we're here to explore.

In this book, we're going to take a journey together through the evolution of change management, from its rigid beginnings to the fluid, human-centric approaches of today. We'll explore why traditional models fall short in our dynamic business environment and introduce you to a new paradigm—Human-Centric Change Management.

Get ready to discover how you can marry the best of Agile practices with a deep understanding of human psychology to create a change management approach that's as nimble as it is empathetic. By the time you finish this book, you'll have a tool kit of strategies to not just manage change but also embrace it and thrive in it, allowing you to lead your organization confidently into the future.

> So, are you ready to become a leader of change? Let's dive in!

1

Change Is Hard

Change, a constant in both life and business, is inherently difficult for individuals and organizations alike. Despite its inevitability and frequent necessity, there is often significant resistance and many obstacles to the process of change.

Why Don't People Change?

Simply put, change is hard because it disrupts the status quo. Humans are creatures of habit, finding comfort and security in familiar routines and established ways of doing things. This preference for the familiar is deeply rooted in our psychology, stemming from our evolutionary past, where predictability often meant safety. In an organizational context, this translates to employees feeling threatened by changes that alter their daily routines, challenge their expertise, or potentially jeopardize their position within the company.

This is further compounded by the fear of the unknown. When faced with change, individuals often focus on potentially negative outcomes rather than possible benefits. This negativity bias can lead to anxiety, stress, and active resistance to new initiatives. In organizations, this manifests as employees clinging to outdated processes or technologies, even when they're clearly inefficient, simply because they're familiar and predictable.

Another factor that makes change challenging is the effort required to learn new skills or adapt to new systems. The human brain is wired to conserve energy, and learning requires significant cognitive resources. This can lead to mental fatigue and frustration, especially when changes are frequent or complex. In a business setting, this can result in lower productivity during transitional periods and resistance from employees who feel overwhelmed by the demands of adapting to new ways of working.

Change is also difficult because it often involves loss. Even positive changes can involve letting go of familiar aspects of one's job or work environment. This sense of loss can trigger a grief-like response, with individuals going through stages of denial, anger, and bargaining before acceptance. In organizations, this emotional process can slow down change initiatives and create a negative atmosphere that affects morale and productivity.

The social dynamics within organizations add another layer of complexity to change. Established power structures, informal networks, and team dynamics can all be disrupted by significant changes. Those who benefit from the current system may actively resist changes that threaten their status or influence. This political dimension of change can lead to conflict, power struggles, and the formation of opposing factions within the organization, further complicating the change process.

What Happens When People Don't Change?

Understanding why change is hard is crucial, but equally important is recognizing the consequences of remaining stuck in the status quo. Organizations that fail to adapt to shifting market conditions, evolving customer needs, or technological advancements risk becoming obsolete. The business landscape is littered with once-dominant companies that failed to change in the face of disruption, from Kodak's struggle with the shift to digital photography to Blockbuster's inability to adapt to streaming services.

When organizations resist change, they often experience a gradual decline in performance. Outdated processes and technologies lead to inefficiencies, increasing costs and reducing productivity. This can result in a loss of competitive advantage as more Agile competitors become better at meeting market demands. Over time, this performance gap can widen, making it increasingly difficult for the organization to catch up, even if it eventually decides to change.

Failure to embrace change can also significantly impact employee morale and engagement. Top talent, particularly younger workers, are often drawn to dynamic, forward-thinking organizations. When a company is perceived as stagnant or resistant to change, it may struggle to attract and retain skilled employees. This can lead to a brain drain, with the most adaptable and innovative staff leaving for more progressive organizations, further hampering the company's ability to compete and evolve.

Resistance to change can create a culture of complacency within an organization. When employees see that the status quo is preserved despite clear needs for improvement, they may become disengaged and stop offering innovative ideas or solutions. This can stifle creativity and problem-solving, leaving the organization ill-equipped to manage challenges or capitalize on opportunities.

An organization's reputation with customers and stakeholders may also take a hit in this scenario. In today's fast-paced business climate, customers expect companies to continuously improve their products, services, and customer experience. Those that fail to evolve risk being perceived as outdated or out of touch, potentially losing customers to more innovative competitors.

Furthermore, resistance to change can create misalignment between an organization and its external environment. As markets evolve, customer preferences shift, and innovative technologies emerge; organizations that don't adapt can find themselves increasingly out of step with the realities of their industry. This misalignment can lead to missed opportunities and an increasing disconnect between the organization's offerings and market demands.

While businesses and organizations often focus on the strategic and operational aspects of driving change, it is all too easy to overlook the human element. This can prove to be a critical misstep, as some of the greatest barriers to successful change often arise from the very people that change is intended to impact.

Illustration

Consider the case of ForgeSmiths, a long-standing producer of industrial equipment. After years of steady growth, the company found itself facing increased global competition and a need to modernize its operations. The leadership team developed a comprehensive plan to automate key processes, upgrade technology systems, and realign the workforce to drive greater efficiencies.

On paper, the changes made strategic and financial sense. However, the executives failed to adequately account for the human impact. The automation initiatives were viewed by many factory workers as a threat to their livelihoods. The new technology systems felt confusing and overwhelming to employees accustomed to long-established workflows. And the workforce realignment led to uncertainty, anxiety, and resentment among staff who feared for their job security.

Rather than embracing the proposed changes, a significant portion of the ForgeSmiths workforce rejected them. Productivity plummeted as workers engaged in "passive resistance," finding ways to work around new systems and processes. Morale tanked, with many top performers seeking opportunities elsewhere. In the end, the ambitious transformation plan stalled, with the company struggling to recoup its investments and recover lost ground.

This cautionary tale reminds us that successful change does not occur in a vacuum. People are the heart and soul of any organization, and their thoughts, feelings, and behaviors can make or break even the most meticulously planned initiatives. By overlooking the human element and failing to meaningfully engage and support employees through periods of upheaval, well-intentioned leaders run the risk of inadvertently sabotaging their own change efforts. Only by prioritizing the people side of change can organizations hope to navigate the turbulent waters of transformation and emerge stronger on the other side.

Call to Action

While change is undeniably challenging, the consequences of ignoring what needs to be done can be far more severe. The difficulties associated with change—from psychological resistance to the practical challenges of implementation—are significant but surmountable with the right approach and mindset. Organizations must recognize that change, despite its challenges, is essential for growth, innovation, and long-term survival.

Companies that understand why change is hard and actively work to overcome these obstacles can position themselves to thrive in an ever-evolving business landscape. The ability to navigate and embrace change effectively is not just a valuable skill—it's a critical competency for any organization aiming to succeed in today's dynamic and competitive environment.

> **So, are you ready to face the challenge?**

2

Change Management from 1950 to Now

Change management is a complex but systematic approach to dealing with change from the perspective of both the organization and the individual. The goal of change management is to implement strategies for effecting change, controlling change, and helping people adapt to change. It's about preparing, supporting, and helping individuals, teams, and entire organizations as they transform.

The Need to Oversee Change

Why should we care about change management? Well, it should empower an organization to reach its goals with solutions aligned to its business strategy. However, there's a problem with many of today's change management methods and models: they often put too much emphasis on "control" and being "systematic."

This can lead to several issues:

- **Ineffective Leadership:** Leaders may become too focused on the process rather than inspiring and guiding their teams.

- **Poor Communication:** The emphasis on control can lead to top-down communication that doesn't effectively engage employees.

- **Active and/or Passive Resistance:** When people feel change is being imposed on them without their input, they're more likely to resist.

- **Inadequate Planning:** Ironically, the focus on being systematic can sometimes lead to rigid plans that don't account for the unpredictable nature of change.

- **Lack of Participation:** If employees aren't involved in the change process, they're less likely to buy into it.

- **Neglected Stakeholders:** Some stakeholders may be overlooked in an overly systematic approach.

- **No Opportunities to Learn:** A rigid change management process doesn't allow for learning and adaptation along the way.

These issues highlight why we need a more flexible, human-centric approach to change management—one that balances the need for structure with the realities of human behavior and the fast-paced, unpredictable nature of modern business landscapes.

Before we jump into the brave new world of Human-Centric Change Management, let's take a quick trip down memory lane. To know where you're going, it helps to know where you've been!

The 1950s: The Freeze-Thaw Model

The foundations of modern change management can be traced back to Kurt Lewin, a German American psychologist who developed a three-step model in the 1950s often referred to as Unfreeze-Change-Refreeze.

This model provided a simple yet powerful framework for understanding the process of change in organizations:

- **Unfreeze Stage:** Lewin theorized that organizations must first create the motivation for change by disrupting the existing equilibrium. This involves challenging long-held beliefs and practices, creating a sense of urgency, and preparing employees for the impending change.

- **Change Stage:** This stage represents the transitional period where new behaviors, processes, and structures are introduced and implemented. During this phase, clear communication and support are crucial to help individuals adapt to the new ways of working.

- **Refreeze Stage:** This phase focuses on solidifying and institutionalizing the changes, ensuring they become the new norm within the organization. This involves reinforcing new behaviors, updating policies and procedures, and celebrating successes to embed the changes in the organizational culture.

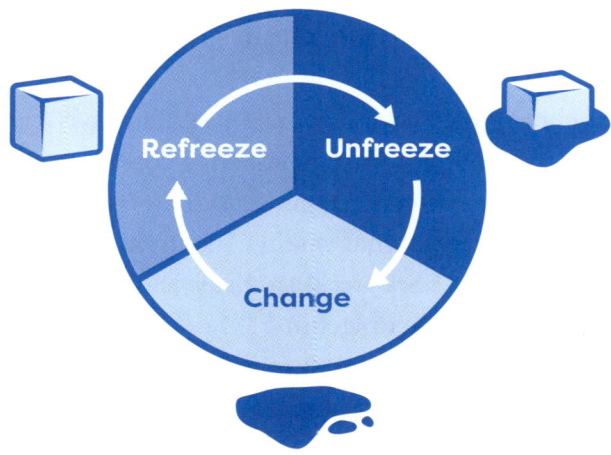

Imagine you're a business leader in the 1950s. The pace of change is glacial compared to today, and Lewin has just introduced his Unfreeze-Change-Refreeze model. It seems perfect—you unfreeze the current state, make your change, and refreeze into the new state. Simple, right?

Fast-forward to today, and you're probably chuckling at the idea of your organization ever being in a "frozen" state. In our current business climate, you're more likely to find a penguin in the Sahara than a company that's not in a constant state of flux!

The PDCA Cycle: A Step in the Right Direction

Concurrent with Lewin's work, Dr. W. Edwards Deming was developing his own approach to change and continuous improvement. Deming, an American engineer, statistician, and management consultant, introduced the Plan-Do-Check-Act (PDCA) cycle, also known as the Deming Cycle or Deming Wheel.

This four-step model for conducting change is aimed at promoting continuous improvement in processes and products.

The four stages are:

1. **Plan:** Identify and analyze the problem or opportunity for improvement. Define goals and develop a plan for achieving them.

2. **Do:** Implement the plan on a small scale or pilot basis. This involves executing the proposed changes and collecting data.

3. **Check:** Evaluate the results by comparing the data to the expected outcomes. Analyze what worked well and what didn't.

4. **Act:** If the change was successful, implement it on a wider scale and standardize the new processes. If not, begin the cycle again with a modified plan.

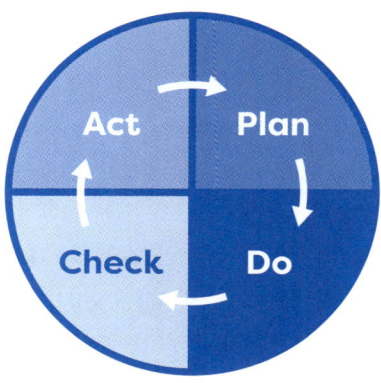

Deming's approach emphasized the importance of iterative learning and constant improvement. While not exclusively focused on organizational change management, the PDCA cycle has been widely adopted in various fields, including business management, healthcare, and education. Its influence can be seen in modern Agile and Lean methods, which prioritize iterative development and continuous improvement.

The PDCA cycle complements other change management models by providing a structured approach to implementing and refining changes. It encourages organizations to test changes on a small scale before full implementation, reducing risk and allowing for adjustments based on real-world feedback.

The 1960s:
Elisabeth Kübler-Ross's Change Curve

Although not originally developed for organizational change, Elisabeth Kübler-Ross's work on the stages of grief in the 1960s has been widely adapted to understand emotional responses to change in the workplace. The Kübler-Ross Change Curve describes the emotional journey individuals typically experience when faced with significant change.

The model outlines five stages: denial, anger, bargaining, depression, and acceptance. In the context of organizational change, employees may initially deny the need for change, then express anger or resistance. This is followed by attempts to negotiate or bargain, potentially leading to a period of low morale or productivity (depression) before they finally accept and embrace the change.

The Kübler-Ross Change Curve:

1. **Denial:** In this initial stage, individuals may react to news of change with disbelief or shock. In an organizational context, employees might dismiss the need for change or assume it won't affect them personally. This defense mechanism allows people to buffer the immediate shock of the change and gradually absorb its reality.

2. **Anger:** As the reality of the change sets in, individuals often experience frustration and anger. This might manifest as resistance to the change, criticism of leadership, or general discontent in the workplace. Employees may question why the change is necessary or feel that it's unfair. This stage is crucial for change managers to address, as unresolved anger can lead to long-term resistance.

3. **Bargaining:** In this stage, individuals attempt to negotiate or find a way out of the impending change. In an organizational setting, this might involve employees trying to delay the implementation of new processes, suggesting alternatives, or seeking compromises. While this can sometimes

lead to constructive dialogue, it can also be a form of resistance if not managed properly.

4. **Depression:** As the change becomes more imminent and bargaining proves ineffective, morale can sink. This stage is characterized by a lack of energy, decreased productivity, and a sense of helplessness. Employees might disengage from their work or express doubts about their ability to adapt to the new situation. This stage, while challenging, often marks the turning point where individuals begin to accept the inevitability of the change.

5. **Acceptance:** In the final stage, individuals come to terms with the change and begin to move forward. This doesn't necessarily mean they're happy about the change, but they've accepted its reality and are ready to adapt. In the workplace, this stage is marked by increased engagement, a willingness to learn new skills, and a focus on the future rather than the past.

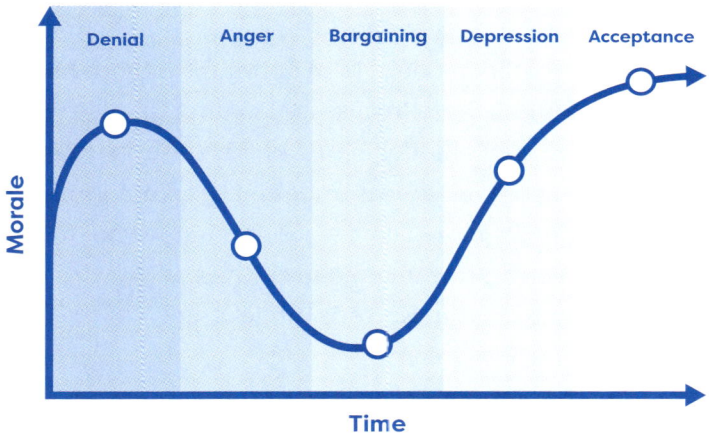

It's important to note that individuals don't always progress through these stages in a linear fashion. People may move back and forth between stages or experience multiple stages simultaneously. The duration and intensity of each stage can vary greatly depending on the individual and the nature of the change.

Understanding this emotional journey has helped humanize change management. Further, anticipating and addressing the psychological impacts of organizational transformations has led to more empathetic and effective change strategies.

The 1990s: Kotter Steps In

Building on earlier models, John Kotter introduced his influential Eight-Step Process for Leading Change in the 1990s. Kotter's model, based on his observations of numerous organizations undergoing transformations, provided a more comprehensive framework for managing large-scale change initiatives.

The eight steps in Kotter's model are:

1. **Create a Sense of Urgency:** Motivating people to recognize the need for change. This step involves making the status quo seem more dangerous than the unknown. Leaders must communicate the critical nature of the change and why it needs to happen now. This might involve sharing market data, competitor analysis, or potential threats to create a compelling case for change.

2. **Build a Guiding Coalition:** Assembling a group with enough power and influence to lead the change effort. This team should represent various departments, levels, and types of expertise within the organization. The coalition needs both the

authority to make decisions and the credibility to be respected by the wider organization.

3. **Form a Strategic Vision and Initiatives:** Creating a clear, compelling vision of the future state. The vision should be easy to communicate and appeal to customers, stakeholders, and employees. It should provide a clear direction for the organization and inspire action. This step also involves developing strategic initiatives to achieve this vision.

4. **Enlist a Volunteer Army:** Communicating the vision and strategy to create buy-in and attract a large group of people willing to drive change. This step is about engaging the broader organization. The vision needs to be communicated frequently and powerfully and be embedded in everything the organization does. Leaders should lead by example, demonstrating the behaviors they're asking of others.

5. **Enable Action by Removing Barriers:** Removing obstacles to change, changing systems or structures that undermine the vision. This

might involve adjusting hierarchies, changing job descriptions, or providing training. The goal is to empower people to execute the vision, encouraging risk-taking and unconventional ideas, activities, and actions.

6. **Generate Short-Term Wins:** Planning for and creating visible, unambiguous successes as soon as possible. Short-term wins provide evidence that sacrifices are worth it, reward agents of change, help fine-tune vision and strategies, undermine cynics, keep bosses on board, and build momentum.

7. **Sustain Acceleration:** Using the credibility gained from early wins to change systems, structures, and policies that don't align with the vision. This step involves hiring, promoting, and developing employees who can implement the vision; reinvigorating the change process with new projects and themes; and maintaining a sense of urgency.

8. **Institute Change:** Anchoring innovative approaches in the organizational culture. For change to stick, it must become part of the core of the

organization. The new behaviors and practices need to be shown to have improved performance. Efforts should be made to ensure leadership development supports the new ways.

Kotter's 8-Step Change Model

Kotter's approach emphasized the critical role of leadership in driving change, the importance of creating a shared vision, and the need for sustained effort to embed changes in organizational culture. His model remains widely used and has been adapted by many organizations facing significant transformations.

The eight steps are more comprehensive than their predecessors but still assume change is a linear process with a clear start and end point. In today's world, you know that change is more like a never-ending game of Whac-A-Mole!

The 2000s: Enter ADKAR

As the field of change management continued to evolve, Jeff Hiatt introduced the ADKAR model in the early 2000s. ADKAR, which stands for Awareness, Desire, Knowledge, Ability, and Reinforcement, is a goal-oriented approach to an individual's journey through change.

The five elements of ADKAR represent the steps an individual must take to successfully adopt and sustain a change:

1. Awareness of the need for change.

2. Desire to support and participate in the change.

3. Knowledge of how to change.

4. Ability to implement required skills and behaviors.

5. Reinforcement to sustain the change.

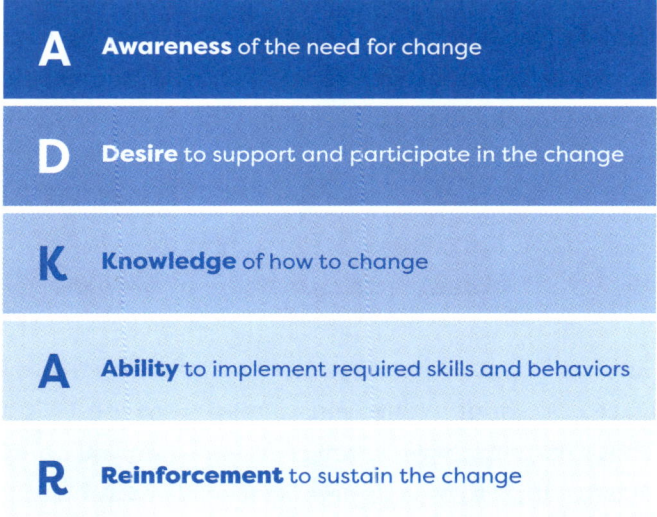

Hiatt's model emphasizes the importance of addressing each of these elements sequentially to ensure successful change in individuals, which in turn drives organizational change. The ADKAR model has been widely adopted due to its practicality and focus on measurable outcomes.

While it acknowledges the human element, ADKAR still doesn't quite capture the fluid nature of modern change. It does not adequately address broader organizational factors, resistance to change, or long-term sustainability. Additionally, the ADKAR model's linear nature and limited focus on group dynamics and cultural considerations can be problematic in diverse, global organizations.

The Problem with Traditional Models

So what's the real issue? Well, imagine trying to navigate rush-hour traffic using a map from the 1950s. That's essentially what you're doing when you apply these models to today's organizational environment. They're too rigid, too linear, and they don't account for the constant state of flux that defines modern business.

Moreover, they often overlook a crucial factor—the human element. Your employees aren't robots that can be reprogrammed at will. They have emotions, fears, and individual motivations that play a huge role in how they approach change.

Illustration

In the heart of the Midwest, Heartland Power & Light (HP&L) stood as a testament to reliability and tradition. Founded in the 1930s, this utility company had weathered decades of technological advancements and regulatory shifts. However, as the energy landscape began to transform rapidly in the twenty-first century, HP&L found itself grappling with the limitations of its long-standing approach to change management.

For decades, HP&L had relied on change management methodologies rooted in the industrial era. The company's leadership, many of whom had risen through the ranks since the 1970s and '80s, clung to the familiar top-down, command-and-control approaches popularized in the mid-twentieth century.

When faced with the need to modernize its grid infrastructure and integrate renewable energy sources in the early 2010s, HP&L's executive team dusted off their well-worn playbook. They began by crafting a detailed five-year plan, complete with rigidly defined milestones and a cascade of directives to be implemented across the organization.

The change process kicked off with a company-wide memo, followed by a series of formal presentations where managers explained the new initiatives to their teams. The approach mirrored the linear, step-by-step models popularized by change management theorists of the 1950s and '60s, such as Kurt Lewin's Unfreeze-Change-Refreeze model.

However, as HP&L attempted to roll out its modernization efforts, the limitations of this outdated approach became glaringly apparent. The younger, tech-savvy engineers found the rigid, top-down communication style alienating and unrelatable. They craved more collaborative, dynamic ways of working that allowed for rapid experimentation and iteration.

Meanwhile, longtime field technicians, accustomed to decades of stable processes, felt overwhelmed by the scope and pace of change. The company's traditional change management approach offered little in the way of emotional support or opportunities for these employees to voice their concerns and contribute their valuable experiential knowledge.

As the project progressed, HP&L's leadership found themselves constantly behind schedule and over budget. The meticulously planned milestones proved unrealistic in the face of rapidly evolving technology and shifting regulatory landscapes. The company's inability to adapt quickly left it struggling to keep pace with more Agile competitors entering the market.

Furthermore, the traditional emphasis on managing resistance to change through compliance and control measures backfired spectacularly. Instead of embracing the new technologies and processes, many employees found creative ways to work around them, clinging to familiar methods that felt more comfortable and reliable.

By the mid-2010s, HP&L's modernization efforts were in disarray. Employee morale had plummeted, customer satisfaction was at an all-time low, and the company faced mounting pressure from regulators and shareholders to accelerate its transformation.

This crisis forced HP&L's leadership to confront an uncomfortable truth: their tried-and-true change management methods, rooted in mid-twentieth-century industrial paradigms, were woefully inadequate for navigating the complex, fast-paced realities of the modern energy sector.

The HP&L story serves as a stark example of how change management approaches that once served organizations well can become liabilities in a rapidly evolving business landscape. It highlights the pressing need for a more adaptive, human-centric approach to change—one that recognizes the complexities of modern work environments, embraces the diverse perspectives and needs of a multigenerational workforce, and remains flexible enough to navigate the unpredictable currents of technological and social change.

As HP&L and countless other organizations have discovered, successfully navigating change requires more than just updating the content of our change initiatives. It demands a fundamental rethinking of how we approach the process of change itself.

Call to Action

The field of change management has come a long way since Kurt Lewin's groundbreaking work in the 1950s.

Each subsequent model, from Deming's PDCA cycle to Hiatt's ADKAR model, has contributed valuable insights into the complex process of organizational change. These frameworks have provided structure, guidance, and a common language for leaders and change practitioners to navigate the turbulent waters of transformation.

However, as our understanding of organizational dynamics and human behavior has deepened, certain limitations of traditional change management models have become apparent. One significant issue is the inherent linearity of many of these models. While they often acknowledge that change is not always a straightforward process, their step-by-step nature can create an illusion of predictability in what is often a messy, nonlinear journey. This can lead to frustration and a sense of failure when organizations don't neatly progress through predetermined stages.

Another challenge is the tendency of these models to focus primarily on top-down, planned change initiatives. In today's rapidly evolving business environment, change is often emergent, arising from various levels within the organization or in response to external factors. Traditional models may struggle to account for this bottom-up or spontaneous change, potentially overlooking valuable innovations and adaptations that occur outside formal change processes.

Many traditional models also underestimate the impact of organizational culture and informal networks when making changes. While culture is often mentioned as a factor, it's frequently treated as something that can be managed or altered through a series of steps rather than as a complex, deeply rooted aspect of organizational life that both influences and is influenced by change initiatives.

Furthermore, these models often assume a relatively stable external environment during the change process. In reality, organizations today operate in a state of constant flux, with multiple changes occurring simultaneously and new challenges emerging before previous ones are fully addressed. This dynamic context can make it difficult to apply models that assume a clear beginning and end to change initiatives.

The emotional and psychological aspects of change, while acknowledged in models like the Kübler-Ross Change Curve, are sometimes oversimplified. The complex interplay of individual experiences, team dynamics, and organizational context can create a wide array of responses to change that may not fit neatly into predefined stages or categories.

Additionally, many traditional models were developed in a Western, primarily American, business context. As organizations become increasingly global and diverse, these models may not fully account for cultural differences in how change is perceived, communicated, and implemented across different societies and organizational cultures.

Remember, as George Bernard Shaw once said, "Progress is impossible without change, and those who cannot change their minds cannot change anything."

> So, are you ready to change your mind about change management?

3

The Problem(s) to Be Solved

The history and evolution of change management show us why there's a need for a more adaptive, human-centric approach to the field that can keep up with the pace of modern business while still focusing on the crucial human element of change.

As you've navigated the choppy waters of transformation and growth within your organization, you've likely noticed that traditional change management models often fall short.

The Problem: One Size Doesn't Fit All

One of the most glaring issues with traditional change management is its rigid, one-size-fits-all approach. There is often a set series of steps to be followed sequentially, regardless of the unique context of the organization or the specific nature of the change being implemented. This inflexibility can lead to a disconnect between the change strategy and the actual needs of the organization and its employees. As a result, change initiatives may fail to address crucial aspects of the transformation, leaving gaps that can undermine the entire process.

The rigidity of traditional approaches can have far-reaching negative impacts on organizations. It can stifle innovation and creativity, as employees are discouraged from suggesting alternative methods or solutions that don't fit within the prescribed change model. This can lead to missed opportunities for improvement and a failure to leverage the collective intelligence of the workforce. Moreover, inflexibility can result in change initiatives that are poorly aligned with the organization's culture and values, leading to resistance and low adoption rates.

Another significant problem with traditional change management is its overemphasis on top-down communication and implementation as we have previewed above. This approach often assumes that change can be effectively cascaded down through the organizational hierarchy, with leadership making decisions and employees simply following instructions. This neglect of bottom-up input can lead to a sense of disempowerment among employees, fostering resentment and resistance to change.

The negative impact of this top-down approach is profound. It can create a divide between leadership and employees, eroding trust and damaging organizational culture. Employees may feel that their expertise and insights are undervalued, leading to decreased engagement and motivation. They may only comply superficially with change initiatives rather than genuinely adopt and internalize new practices or mindsets. This can lead to the failure of change initiatives or, at best, suboptimal results that fall short of the organization's goals.

Traditional change management also often fails to adequately address the emotional and psychological aspects of change. It tends to focus primarily on the rational and logistical elements of transformation, overlooking the fact that change is fundamentally a human process. This can mean that employees are not given the support they need to navigate the emotional challenges associated with change, such as uncertainty, fear, and loss.

As we have seen, this neglect of the human element

can have severe consequences for organizations. It can lead to increased stress and burnout among employees, resulting in decreased productivity and higher turnover rates. The workforce may become less resilient and adaptable, leaving the organization ill-prepared for future changes. Furthermore, by failing to address the psychological aspects of change, organizations may miss opportunities to build stronger, more cohesive teams during periods of transition.

Traditional change management often sets unrealistic timelines and expectations, assuming that change can be implemented quickly and cleanly with a clear start and end point. This fails to recognize that meaningful organizational change is typically a messy, nonlinear process that requires ongoing adjustment and refinement.

Unrealistic expectations can be detrimental to organizations. They can lead to rushed implementations that don't allow sufficient time for learning and adaptation. This can result in half-baked changes that fail to deliver the intended benefits or, worse, create new problems within the organization. The pressure to meet unrealistic deadlines can also increase stress levels among employees and leaders, potentially leading to burnout and decreased quality of work.

Traditional change management also tends to overemphasize formal training and communication at the expense of experiential learning and informal networks. While training and official communications are important, they are often insufficient to drive real behavioral change and skill development. This approach fails to leverage the power of peer-to-peer learning and the informal social structures that exist within organizations.

Overreliance on formal mechanisms reduces the effectiveness of change initiatives. Employees may receive information about the change but lack the practical experience to implement it effectively in their daily work. This can lead to a gap between the intended change and the actual practices within the organization. Additionally, by neglecting informal networks, organizations miss out on the benefits of having natural Change Champions and influencers who could help drive adoption and enthusiasm for the transformation.

Lastly, traditional change management often lacks robust feedback mechanisms and the flexibility to adjust course based on real-time information. As discussed, many traditional approaches assume a linear progression through predetermined stages, with limited opportunity for reassessment and modification along the way. This can result in a failure to identify and address issues as they arise during the change process.

The impact of this lack of adaptability can be severe. Organizations may continue down a path that is clearly not working, wasting resources and damaging morale in the process. The inability to course correct can lead to changes that are no longer relevant or beneficial, as the business environment may have shifted since the initial planning stages. This rigidity can also frustrate employees who see problems but feel powerless to address them, leading to disengagement and cynicism about future change initiatives.

Sustaining Change

While traditional change management approaches have their merits, their limitations can significantly hinder an organization's ability to implement effective and sustainable change. The rigidity, top-down focus, neglect of human factors, unrealistic expectations, overemphasis on formal mechanisms, and lack of adaptability inherent in many traditional approaches can lead to failed change initiatives, wasted resources, damaged organizational culture, and a workforce ill-equipped to manage ongoing transformation. As organizations continue to face increasingly complex and rapid changes, it is crucial to recognize these shortcomings and seek more flexible, human-centric approaches to managing change. Only by addressing these fundamental issues can organizations hope to successfully navigate the choppy waters of modern business and emerge stronger from periods of transformation.

The Need for a Solution

You're right—there must be an answer! The limitations of traditional models necessitate an innovative approach to change management.

This innovative approach needs to be:

- Agile and responsive to rapid change.

- Centered on the human aspects of change.

- Flexible and adaptable.

- Focused on continuous learning and improvement.

- Capable of meeting the complex needs of modern organizations.

Illustration

For decades, the standard playbook for driving organizational change has centered around a top-down, process-oriented methodology. This "command and control" approach typically involves senior leaders formulating a strategic vision, developing a detailed implementation plan, and then cascading directives down through the organizational hierarchy. The assumption is that by rigorously managing the sequence of activities, timelines, and resource requirements, change can be executed in a controlled and predictable manner.

However, the limitations of this conventional wisdom have become increasingly apparent in today's dynamic business environment. Consider the case of Grid Comm, a once-dominant player in the communications industry that found itself facing severe headwinds in the face of rapid technological disruption.

Recognizing the need for a major transformation, the executive team at Grid Comm dutifully followed the established change management playbook. They crafted an ambitious multiyear plan to overhaul the company's technology infrastructure, streamline operations, and realign the workforce. Supported by a team of experienced consultants, they methodically tracked progress against key milestones and implemented rigorous performance management systems to drive accountability.

Yet, despite their best efforts, the change initiative struggled to gain traction. Employees grew increasingly cynical and disengaged, with many resisting the new directives from above. Unforeseen challenges and unanticipated market shifts repeatedly forced the leadership team to adjust their plans, often causing further upheaval and confusion. Morale plummeted, and the company hemorrhaged top talent as people grew weary of the constant state of flux.

Ultimately, Grid Comm's transformation efforts fell far short of their ambitious goals. The company ceded significant ground to nimbler, more innovative competitors and found itself in a precarious strategic position.

In today's complex, fast-paced business environment, the conventional, top-down approach to change management is increasingly ineffective. Rigid, process-first methodologies struggle to keep pace with the speed of change and often fail to adequately address the human dynamics that can make or break transformation efforts. To succeed in this new reality, organizations must evolve their change management practices to be more agile, collaborative, and human centric.

Call to Action

Traditional change management approaches, while valuable in their time, often fall short in addressing the deeply human aspects of change, leading to a cascade of problems that can derail even the most well-intentioned transformation efforts.

Most importantly, traditional change management often overlooks the power of intrinsic motivation and employee agency. By treating employees as passive recipients of change rather than active participants, these approaches miss out on the wealth of knowledge, creativity, and commitment that engaged employees can bring to the transformation process.

As you turn your attention to Human-Centric Change Management, you'll understand how this innovative approach addresses these shortcomings and offers a more effective path forward. By placing people at the heart of change initiatives, organizations can tap into the full potential of their workforce, creating more resilient, adaptive, and innovative cultures.

Human-Centric Change Management promises to bridge the gap between organizational objectives and individual experiences, fostering a sense of ownership and engagement that traditional models often struggle to achieve. It acknowledges the complexity of human emotions and motivations, working with these factors rather than attempting to overcome them. This approach also recognizes change as a continuous process, weaving adaptability into the very fabric of the organization.

> So, are you ready to solve your organization's problem(s)?

4

Transforming Change from Challenge to Opportunity

It's a common adage in the business world that people don't like change. This belief has become so ingrained that it's often accepted as an immutable truth, a hurdle that leaders must simply overcome. However, organizations can create an environment where change is not just tolerated but embraced and even sought after.

The key to fostering a culture that thrives on change lies in understanding human psychology. Resistance to change often stems from fear—fear of the unknown, fear of failure, or fear of losing status or comfort. By addressing these underlying concerns and creating a supportive environment, organizations can shift the narrative around change from one of threat to one of opportunity.

Understanding the Psychology of Change

A fundamental aspect of creating a change-positive culture is building trust. When employees trust their leaders and the organization as a whole, they're more likely to view change initiatives as beneficial rather than threatening. This trust is cultivated through consistent, transparent communication and by demonstrating a genuine commitment to employee well-being throughout the transformation process. Leaders who are open about the reasons for change, honest about potential challenges, and clear about how employees will be supported are more likely to gain buy-in and enthusiasm for new initiatives.

Another crucial element is empowerment. When people feel they have agency in the change process, their resistance often diminishes. This can be achieved by involving employees in the planning and implementation of change initiatives. By soliciting input, encouraging feedback, and allowing teams to shape how changes are implemented in their areas, organizations can transform passive recipients of change into active participants and advocates.

Creating a culture of learning also plays a significant role in fostering a positive attitude toward change. When an organization values continuous learning and growth, change becomes an opportunity for development rather than a threat. This can be reinforced through training programs, mentoring initiatives, and by celebrating when employees successfully adapt to or drive transformation.

Recognition and rewards are powerful ways to shape attitudes toward change. By acknowledging and rewarding individuals and teams who successfully navigate the unknown, embrace new ways of working, or drive innovation, organizations positively reinforce change-oriented behaviors. This doesn't necessarily mean monetary rewards; public recognition, increased responsibilities, or opportunities for career advancement can be equally effective.

It's also important to create a safe environment for experimentation and failure. Fear of failure is a significant barrier to embracing change. By fostering a culture where calculated risks are encouraged and failures are viewed as learning opportunities, organizations can reduce this fear. Such an approach not only makes people more open to change but can also drive innovation and continuous improvement.

The physical work environment can also play a role in creating a change-positive culture. Flexible workspaces that can be easily reconfigured, collaborative areas that encourage cross-functional interaction, and visual management tools that make change initiatives visible and tangible can all contribute to an atmosphere where growth feels natural and ongoing.

The behavior of leaders is perhaps the most critical factor in shaping attitudes toward change. Leaders who model adaptability, demonstrate a willingness to learn and change themselves, and maintain a positive outlook during periods of transformation set the tone for the entire organization. When employees see their leaders embracing change enthusiastically, they're more likely to follow suit.

Creating a culture that embraces change is not about making the process constant or chaotic. Rather, it's about building resilience, adaptability, and a growth mindset throughout the organization. It's about fostering an environment where change is seen as a natural part of growth and success rather than a disruptive force to be feared.

The Opportunity

Human-Centric Change Management plays a crucial role in supporting this culture of embracing change. By placing people at the heart of the change process, this approach addresses the psychological and emotional aspects of transformation that are often overlooked in traditional change management methodologies. It recognizes that successful change is not just about new processes or technologies but about how people experience and internalize these shifts.

By adopting Human-Centric Change Management, organizations can better navigate the complex and rapidly evolving business landscape by creating an environment where change is seen as an opportunity for growth and improvement rather than a threat to be resisted.

Illustration

While change is inherently disruptive and can trigger strong resistance, it need not be viewed solely as a threat. In fact, organizations that can foster a culture of change resilience can harness the power of transformation to unlock new opportunities and sources of competitive advantage.

One such example is Bright Horizons, a leading provider of early childhood education and employer-sponsored childcare services. Several years ago, the company found itself at a crossroads as it grappled with rapid technological advancements, evolving customer demands, and a shifting regulatory landscape.

Rather than responding reactively, the leadership team at Bright Horizons proactively embraced change as a strategic imperative. They engaged employees at all levels to solicit feedback and ideas, recognizing that the frontline staff had invaluable insights into the challenges and pain points experienced by both clients and colleagues. This inclusive, collaborative approach helped cultivate a shared sense of ownership and purpose around the transformation efforts.

Bright Horizons also invested heavily in developing the change management capabilities of its workforce. Employees were provided with comprehensive training on navigating uncertainty, managing stress, and leading through periods of disruption. Periodic "change check-ins" were scheduled to gauge sentiments, address concerns, and celebrate small wins along the way. Importantly, the leadership team modeled the desired behaviors, visibly championing the change agenda and proactively addressing resistance head-on.

Over time, this intentional, people-centric approach transformed Bright Horizons' organizational culture. What was once viewed as a necessary evil gradually came to be seen as an opportunity for growth and innovation. Employees demonstrated increased agility, adaptability, and resilience in the face of ongoing change. Rather than hunkering down, they actively sought out ways to enhance processes, explore new technologies, and better serve customers.

The results speak for themselves. Bright Horizons not only navigated the challenging industry shifts successfully but emerged as an even stronger, more competitive industry leader. Retention rates soared as employees became passionate advocates for the company's transformation agenda. Clients were impressed by the organization's responsiveness and ability to anticipate their evolving needs. Perhaps most importantly, the Bright Horizons team developed a newfound confidence in their collective ability to manage change, welcoming it as a chance to push the boundaries of what was possible.

This inspiring case study illustrates that when change is approached thoughtfully, strategically, and with a keen focus on the human element, it need not be viewed as a necessary evil. Rather, it can serve as a powerful catalyst for unlocking new sources of value, driving innovation, and strengthening organizational resilience. By cultivating a culture that embraces rather than resists transformation forward-thinking, companies can transform disruption into competitive advantage.

Call to Action

While it's true that change can be challenging, it is entirely possible to create an organizational culture where people not only accept the process but thrive in it. By building trust, empowering employees, fostering a learning culture, recognizing Change Champions, creating safe spaces for experimentation, shaping the physical environment, and ensuring leaders embrace change, organizations can transform their approach. In such an environment, change becomes an exciting journey of growth and opportunity rather than a daunting obstacle to be overcome.

The goal is not to make change easy—it will always require effort and adjustment. Instead, the aim is to make the process rewarding, to create a shared understanding that through change, both individuals and the organization can reach new heights of success and fulfillment. In this way, change becomes not something to be endured but something to be embraced—a catalyst for growth, innovation, and achievement in an ever-evolving world.

> So, are you ready to cultivate a culture of embracing change?

5

A Tale of Two Approaches

Change is hard. People don't change. So how do you pass beyond this theory? As the business world continues to evolve at a breakneck pace, the ability to navigate organizational change is a requirement. Traditional approaches to change management have proven increasingly ineffective in the face of rapid technological disruption, shifting customer expectations, and the ever-changing needs of the modern workforce. Change is how you put theory to the test!

Traditional versus Human-Centric Change Management

Leaders have long sought to develop effective strategies for navigating the complex landscape of transformation. Traditionally, the field of change management has been dominated by top-down, process-oriented methodologies rooted in the seminal works of theorists like Kurt Lewin and John Kotter. These conventional approaches emphasize the importance of establishing a clear vision, developing a detailed implementation plan, and rigorously managing the sequence of activities and timelines to drive change in a controlled, predictable manner.

However, as the pace of business has accelerated and the nature of work has become increasingly dynamic, the limitations of this traditional change management paradigm have become increasingly apparent. As Prosci, a leading change management research and training organization, has noted, "Change is no longer an event, but an ongoing capability that organizations must develop." In today's complex, disruption-prone environment, the rigid, linear models of the past often struggle to keep up.

Enter the concept of Human-Centric Change Management—an emerging approach that places the needs, fears, and aspirations of the workforce at the heart of transformation efforts. Grounded in the principles of design thinking, organizational development, and positive psychology, this people-focused methodology challenges the conventional wisdom that change can be neatly engineered and imposed from above.

Instead, Human-Centric Change Management emphasizes the importance of active employee engagement, transparent communication, and an adaptive, iterative mindset. Rather than rolling out a predetermined plan, leaders are encouraged to continually solicit feedback, experiment with new approaches, and empower frontline teams to drive continuous improvement.

Importantly, this shift in perspective does not negate the value of rigorous planning and process management—rather, it seeks to strike a more balanced, holistic approach. As McKinsey & Company has noted, "The best change programs reinforce core business objectives with an equal emphasis on the organizational and individual changes required."

By weaving together the analytical rigor of traditional change management and the people-centric focus of the human-centric approach, organizations can cultivate a more agile, responsive, and resilient transformation capability. This blended methodology enables leaders to navigate uncertainty with greater clarity, leverage the collective intelligence of the workforce, and foster a culture of change readiness that is essential in today's dynamic business landscape.

Research has shown that this human-centric approach can yield tangible, bottom-line results. A study by Prosci found that organizations that effectively engage and support their employees through change initiatives are 3.5 times more likely to meet or exceed their project objectives. Similarly, a McKinsey analysis revealed that companies that prioritize the people side of change are up to 30 percent more likely to see sustained change over time.

Illustration

GlobalTech, a multinational technology corporation, found itself at a crossroads. For years, the company had prided itself on its innovative products and cutting-edge technology. However, a recent series of customer satisfaction surveys revealed a troubling trend: despite the quality of their products, customers were increasingly frustrated with the company's lack of responsiveness and poor communication.

The Problem

The executive team at GlobalTech realized that to remain competitive, they needed to instill a company-wide culture of customer-centricity. This wasn't just about implementing new processes or technologies; it required a fundamental shift in how every employee approached their work and interacted with customers. The challenge was clear: How could they transform the behaviors and mindsets of over 50,000 employees spread across multiple countries and diverse roles?

Initially, GlobalTech's leadership turned to their traditional change management playbook. They created a top-down communication plan, developed a new set of customer service protocols, and scheduled mandatory training sessions for all employees. The CEO announced the initiative in a company-wide email, emphasizing the importance of putting customers first and outlining the new expectations.

However, after several months, it became apparent that this approach wasn't yielding the desired results. While employees were going through the motions of the new protocols, there was little genuine change in their attitudes or behaviors. Customer satisfaction scores showed only marginal improvement, and employee engagement surveys indicated growing frustration and burnout.

Recognizing the need for a different approach, GlobalTech's chief people officer, Maria Sanchez, proposed a shift to Human-Centric Change Management. She argued that to truly transform the company's culture, they needed to focus on the experiences, motivations, and concerns of their employees.

The first step in this new approach was to conduct a series of empathy workshops across all levels of the organization. These sessions weren't just about discussing customer needs; they were designed to help employees connect with their own experiences as customers and to understand how their work impacted the overall customer experience.

Instead of dictating new behaviors, the change team worked with employees to cocreate a vision of customer-centricity that resonated with their values and aspirations. They encouraged employees to share stories of exceptional customer service they had experienced or provided, using these narratives to build a collective understanding of what great customer-centricity looked like in practice.

The training approach was completely overhauled. Rather than generic customer service scripts, employees participated in immersive simulations that allowed them to experience the customer journey firsthand. These exercises were followed by reflective discussions where employees could share their insights and brainstorm improvements.

Leadership played a crucial role in this new approach. Executives were asked to spend time on the front lines, interacting directly with customers and employees. They shared their experiences and learnings openly, demonstrating vulnerability and a genuine commitment to change.

The company also implemented a peer-to-peer recognition program, where employees could highlight colleagues who exemplified customer-centric behaviors. These stories were shared widely, creating a positive-reinforcement loop and helping to embed the new behaviors into the company culture.

To address the diverse needs of their global workforce, GlobalTech created a network of Culture Champions—employees who volunteered to help tailor the change initiative to local contexts and provide ongoing support to their colleagues. This decentralized approach allowed for greater flexibility and relevance across different regions and departments.

As the Human-Centric Change Management approach took hold, GlobalTech began to see significant shifts in both employee behavior and customer satisfaction. Employees reported feeling more engaged and empowered, with a clearer understanding of how their work contributed to the customer experience. Customer satisfaction scores started to climb steadily, and the company saw an increase in repeat business and positive word-of-mouth referrals.

The transformation wasn't without its challenges. It took longer than the original timeline had anticipated, and there were moments of doubt and setback. However, by staying committed to the human-centric approach and remaining responsive to employee feedback, GlobalTech was able to navigate these obstacles and emerge stronger.

The Outcome

GlobalTech's journey illustrates the profound impact of Human-Centric Change Management in driving behavioral change across a large, complex organization. By focusing on the human elements of change—emotions, motivations, and personal experiences—the company was able to achieve a deeper and more sustainable transformation than traditional methods could have produced.

The benefits of this approach extended beyond the initial goal of improving customer-centricity. GlobalTech saw improvements in employee engagement, interdepartmental collaboration, and overall organizational agility. The company had not only changed its approach to customers but also created a more resilient and adaptive culture.

Perhaps most importantly, this experience transformed how GlobalTech approached all future change initiatives. The company learned that by putting its people at the center of change efforts, it could turn challenges into opportunities for growth and innovation. This shift in perspective positioned GlobalTech not just as a technology leader but as a pioneer in creating a truly human-centric organization ready to thrive in an ever-changing business landscape.

Call to Action

As the pace of change continues to accelerate, the need for organizations to develop a more human-centric approach to transformation has never been more pressing. By prioritizing the needs and experiences of their workforce, leaders can unlock remarkable levels of creativity, collaboration, and resilience—qualities that are essential to navigating the challenges and opportunities of the modern marketplace.

While the traditional models of change management have served a purpose in the past, the complex, disruption-prone environment of today demands a more flexible, adaptive approach. By blending the analytical rigor of conventional methodologies with the people-focused principles of the human-centric paradigm, organizations can cultivate a transformation capability that is both strategically sound and deeply aligned with the needs of their most valuable asset—their people.

Ultimately, the choice between traditional and Human-Centric Change Management is not an either/or proposition. The most successful organizations will be those that can seamlessly integrate these complementary approaches, creating a powerful synthesis that empowers their workforce, drives sustainable change, and positions them for long-term competitive advantage.

> So, are you ready to experiment with an innovative approach?

6

Human-Centric Change Management (Unpacked)

Human-Centric Change Management emerged in the early twenty-first century as a response to the shortcomings of traditional change management approaches. As organizations grappled with increasingly complex and rapid transformations, it became evident that conventional methods often failed to address the human element adequately.

Change initiatives frequently encountered resistance, low adoption rates, and unsustainable results. Recognizing these challenges, forward-thinking practitioners and researchers began to explore ways to place people at the heart of organizational change. This shift in focus gave birth to Human-Centric Change Management, which prioritizes the experiences, needs, and perspectives of individuals affected by change.

Human-Centric Change Management differs from

traditional approaches in several key ways: it prioritizes people's experiences and emotions rather than processes and structures; it's collaborative and iterative rather than top-down and linear; and it is more adaptable to rapid, continuous change compared to rigid, traditional models.

There's also a greater emphasis on continuous learning and adaptation. Human-centric methods prioritize widespread engagement and empowerment, not just communication from the top. While traditional methods often focus on process metrics, human-centric approaches also measure emotional and behavioral changes.

Human Behavior and Change

By acknowledging the fundamental role of human emotions, motivations, and behaviors in the change process, this approach aims to create more effective, sustainable, and meaningful transformations.

Human-Centric Change Management doesn't have a single creator; rather, it has evolved from various theories and practices over the past few decades.

Key contributors include:

- **John Kotter:** His work on leading change emphasized the importance of creating a sense of urgency and building a guiding coalition.

- **Chip and Dan Heath:** Their books *Switch: How to Change Things When Change Is Hard* and *Made to Stick: Why Some Ideas Survive and Others Die* introduced the concept of appealing to both the rational and emotional sides of individuals during change.

- **Jonathan Haidt:** His "Rider and Elephant" metaphor in *The Happiness Hypothesis* provided a framework for understanding the interplay between rational and emotional decision-making.

- **Dr. Ahmed Sidky:** His concept of "Building the Herd" in business agility emphasized the social aspects of change.

- **David Rock:** His work on neuroleadership has shed light on how the brain responds to change.

I imagine Human-Centric Change Management using the following illustration. Let's break it down ...

Human-Centric Change Management

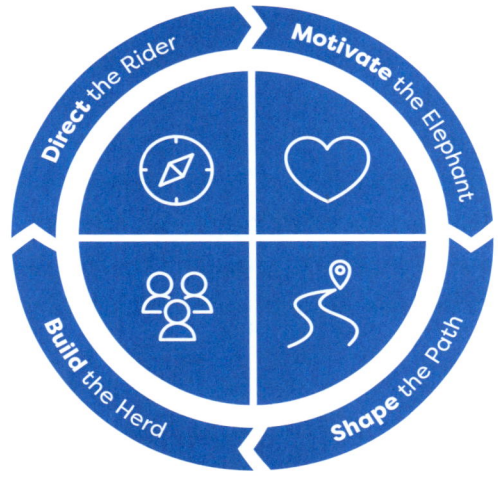

The Rider and the Elephant

Jonathan Haidt's metaphor from *The Happiness Hypothesis* provides a powerful framework for understanding human behavior during change. As Haidt writes, "The mind is divided, like a rider on an elephant, and the rider's job is to serve the elephant." While going through change, our job is to ensure that both the rider and the elephant are aligned and moving in the same direction, toward a better future for the organization and its people.

The rider represents our conscious, reasoning mind—the part of us that plans, analyzes, and makes deliberate choices. While emotions often play a significant role in decision-making, the rider's input is crucial for sustainable change. By appealing to logic and providing clear direction, you can harness the power of rational thinking to overcome resistance and propel change forward.

The elephant represents our unconscious, intuitive mind—the part of us that feels, reacts, and often drives our behavior without conscious thought. While rational arguments are important, it's the elephant that often determines whether change initiatives succeed or fail. By acknowledging and working with our emotional responses, we can create momentum and overcome the inertia that often derails transformation efforts.

To effectively motivate the elephant, leaders must first recognize the power of emotions in decision-making and behavior. Humans are not purely rational beings; our feelings often guide our actions more than our logical thoughts. This understanding is fundamental to creating change strategies that resonate on an emotional level.

Directing the Rider, Motivating the Elephant

Building on Haidt's metaphor, in *Switch: How to Change Things When Change Is Hard*, Chip and Dan Heath offer a compelling model for addressing both the logical and emotional aspects of change: direct the rider; motivate the elephant.

The Heath brothers' model builds on Haidt's metaphor of the rider (our rational side) and the elephant (our emotional side). Successful change requires a delicate balance of guiding the analytical mind while simultaneously engaging the heart.

Directing the rider involves providing crystal-clear guidance to the rational part of our minds. Leaders must articulate a precise destination and a well-defined path to reach it. This clarity is crucial because when faced with ambiguity, the rider tends to spin its wheels, analyzing endlessly without making progress. By breaking down the change process into specific, actionable steps, leaders can give the rider a sense of control and direction.

Before implementing any change initiative, pause and answer these critical questions:

- What's the purpose for the change?

- What's the benefit of implementing the change?

- What outcomes are we expecting to achieve?

However, clear direction alone is not enough. The elephant—our emotional side—also needs to be motivated to move in the desired direction.

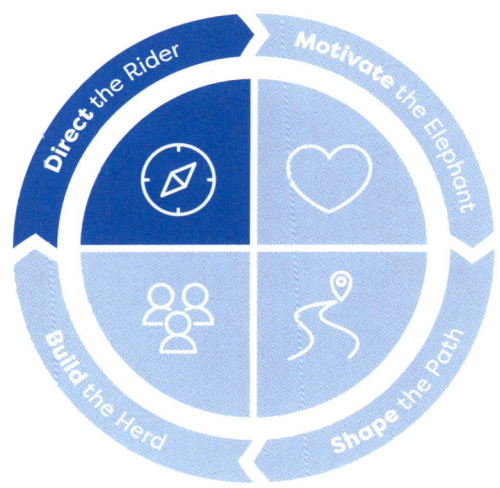

Motivating the elephant involves tapping into the power of emotions to create a genuine desire for change. One effective strategy is appealing to people's values, aspirations, and sense of identity. Leaders should craft a compelling vision of the future that resonates on an emotional level, making people feel excited and inspired about the possibilities that lie ahead.

Another crucial aspect of motivating the elephant is addressing the fears and anxieties that often accompany change. The elephant is naturally resistant to change due to the comfort of familiar routines and the fear of the unknown. Leaders must acknowledge these concerns openly and provide emotional support throughout the process. By creating a sense of psychological safety and demonstrating empathy, they can help soothe the elephant's anxieties and build trust.

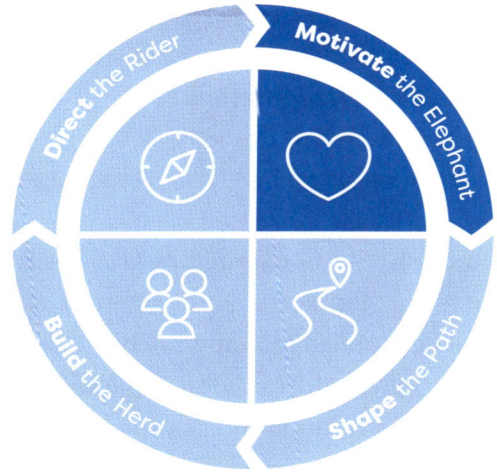

The Heath brothers also emphasize the importance of shrinking change—making the desired behaviors more manageable and less daunting. By breaking down large-scale transformations into smaller, achievable steps, leaders can create a sense of progress and momentum. Each small win motivates the elephant to keep moving forward, building confidence and enthusiasm for the larger change initiative.

To determine if you're truly connecting with emotion, ask yourself these essential questions:

- Who will the change impact?

- What should people know about the change that will excite and delight them?

- How can we inspire people to believe in the change?

It's important to note that directing the rider and motivating the elephant are not separate processes but should be pursued in tandem. The most effective change strategies address both aspects simultaneously, creating a harmonious approach that appeals to both reason and emotion.

As the Heath brothers write, "For individuals' behavior to change, you've got to influence not only their environment but their hearts and minds." This encapsulates the essence of their model—a holistic strategy that addresses the full spectrum of human nature in the pursuit of meaningful and lasting change.

Creating Sustainable, Meaningful Change

In *Made to Stick*, the Heath brothers further refine their model by providing valuable insights into how leaders can shape the path to facilitate desired behaviors and drive successful change initiatives.

One key aspect of **shaping the path** is removing obstacles that hinder the desired change. These obstacles can be physical, procedural, or psychological. For instance, if an organization aims to promote more collaborative work, physical barriers between departments might be removed or shared spaces created. If the goal is to encourage the use of a new software system, ensuring easy access and providing readily available support can smooth the path to adoption.

It is crucial to introduce prompts and triggers that remind people of the desired behaviors. These can be visual cues, reminders, or even subtle changes in the workflow that nudge individuals toward new ways of working. For example, if a company wants to promote sustainability, placing recycling bins in prominent locations with signs explaining how to sort waste properly can serve as a constant reminder of the desired behavior.

The Heath brothers also emphasize the power of habit formation in driving sustainable change. By creating routines and rituals that align with the desired behaviors, leaders can help embed new practices into the organizational culture. This might involve establishing regular check-ins, creating new meeting formats, or introducing rituals that reinforce the change objectives.

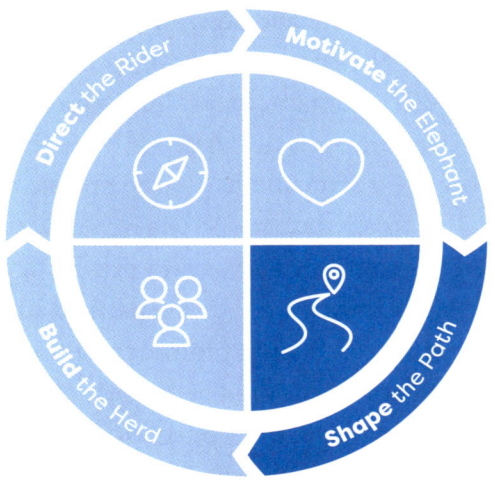

The concept of shaping the path is a powerful tool for Human-Centric Change Management. By focusing on environmental design, removing obstacles, introducing prompts, building habits, using action triggers, and harnessing social influence, organizations support and encourage the desired change. This model recognizes that sustainable change is not just about individual willpower or top-down directives but about creating an ecosystem where the new behaviors are along the path of least resistance.

To craft an environment where change flourishes naturally, consider these crucial questions:

- What clarity needs to be provided?

- What impediments will need to be removed to achieve success?

- What cultural norms could be violated and need to be nurtured?

Leaders who master the art of environmental design will find their initiatives gaining momentum and sustainability in ways that traditional approaches often fail to achieve.

Building the Herd

Dr. Ahmed Sidky's concept of "building the herd" adds a crucial social dimension to change management: humans are inherently social creatures and, as Dr. Sidky states, "Change is a team sport. It's not about changing one person at a time, but about creating a movement where people want to be part of the change."

We look to our peers for cues on how to behave, what to believe, and how to react to new situations. In the context of organizational change, this means that the adoption of new practices or mindsets by individuals is heavily influenced by the perceived behaviors and attitudes of the group.

At its core, **building the herd** is about creating a critical mass of individuals who embrace and embody the desired change. This group serves as a visible example to others, demonstrating that the change is not only possible but beneficial and even desirable. As more people join this "herd," a momentum builds that can carry the entire organization toward the transformation goals.

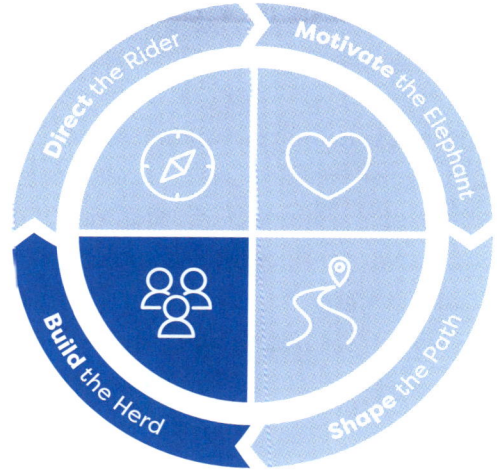

One key aspect of building a herd is identifying and engaging influential members of the organization, often referred to as Change Champions or early adopters. They have the social capital to sway others' opinions and behaviors. By targeting these influencers and gaining their buy-in, leaders can create a ripple effect throughout the organization.

However, it's crucial to note that influence doesn't always flow from the top down. Sometimes, the most impactful advocates for change come from unexpected places within the organizational hierarchy. Dr.

Sidky emphasizes the importance of looking beyond formal leadership structures to find those who truly shape opinions and behaviors at various levels of the organization.

Another vital element of building a herd is creating opportunities for social learning and peer support. This might involve setting up communities of practice, organizing knowledge-sharing sessions, or facilitating mentorship programs. By providing platforms for employees to learn from and support each other through the change process, organizations can accelerate adoption and create a sense of shared experience.

Transparency and visibility play a significant role in this concept. Leaders should strive to highlight the adoption of new practices or mindsets. This might involve showcasing success stories, celebrating milestones, or creating visual representations of progress. When people see their colleagues successfully embracing change, it normalizes the new behaviors and encourages others to follow suit.

It's important to recognize that building a herd is not about creating groupthink or suppressing dissent. Instead, it's about fostering a community that supports and encourages positive change. This community should have space for dialogue, feedback, and even constructive criticism. By creating an environment where people feel safe to express their thoughts and concerns, organizations can build a more resilient and adaptive herd.

The concept also acknowledges the power of social identity. People are more likely to embrace change when they feel it aligns with their sense of who they are and who they want to be. Leaders can tap into this by framing the change in terms of shared values, aspirations, and organizational identity. When people feel that adopting new behaviors or mindsets reinforces their social identity, they're more likely to join the herd willingly.

To ensure you're fostering this collective movement, challenge yourself with these vital questions that illuminate the path forward:

- How are we bridging different perspectives and experiences?

- Who might be falling behind or feeling left out?

- What signals will tell us if someone is disconnecting from the herd?

Why Focus on Human Behavior?

The benefits of adopting a Human-Centric Change Management approach are numerous and far-reaching. Perhaps the most significant advantage is the increased likelihood of success. By actively involving employees in the change process and addressing their concerns and needs, organizations can dramatically reduce resistance to change. When people feel heard, valued, and supported throughout the transformation journey, they are more likely to embrace new ways of working and thinking. This heightened level of engagement leads to smoother transitions and a higher rate of adoption for new processes, technologies, or organizational structures.

Another key benefit of Human-Centric Change Management is the enhancement of employee morale and job satisfaction. Traditional change management approaches often leave employees feeling like passive recipients of change, leading to feelings of powerlessness and frustration. By contrast, Human-Centric Change Management empowers individuals by giving them a voice in the process. When employees are consulted, their ideas are valued, and their concerns are addressed, they develop a sense of ownership over the change. This not only boosts morale but also fosters a more positive work environment, even during significant organizational shifts.

The human-centric approach helps to build a more resilient and adaptable workforce. By focusing on developing the skills and mindsets needed to navigate change effectively, organizations better equip their employees to manage future transformations. This adaptability is crucial in today's fast-paced business environment, where change is constant and unpredictable. Employees who have been through a human-centric change process are more likely to approach future changes with confidence and flexibility rather than fear and resistance.

Improved communication is another significant benefit of Human-Centric Change Management. This approach emphasizes transparent, two-way dialogue throughout the change process. By creating open channels for communication, organizations can quickly identify and address concerns, misconceptions, or roadblocks. This improved flow of information not only helps in managing the current change but also builds trust between leadership and employees, which is invaluable for future initiatives.

Organizations that adopt a human-centric

approach often see an increase in innovation and creativity. By creating an environment where employees feel safe to express ideas and take calculated risks, companies tap into the collective intelligence of their workforce. This can lead to unexpected solutions to change-related challenges and can even spark ideas for further improvements beyond the scope of the initial change initiative.

Human-Centric Change Management also strengthens organizational culture. By demonstrating a commitment to employee well-being and development throughout the change process, organizations reinforce values such as respect, collaboration, and continuous learning. This can have far-reaching effects, improving employee retention, attracting top talent, and enhancing the company's reputation in the marketplace.

From a leadership perspective, the human-centric approach fosters the development of more empathetic and effective leaders. Managers who are trained in this approach learn to balance the technical aspects of change with the human elements. They become more attuned to the needs and concerns of their teams, developing stronger relationships and more effective leadership skills that benefit the organization beyond the change initiative.

The benefits of Human-Centric Change Management extend to the bottom line as well. While it may require more up-front investment in terms of time and resources, this approach often leads to more sustainable change with fewer setbacks. The reduced need for rework, the higher adoption rates of new processes or technologies, and the increased productivity that comes from a more engaged workforce all contribute to a stronger return on investment for change initiatives.

Organizations that excel in human-centric change develop a competitive advantage in their ability to adapt quickly and effectively to market shifts. In an era where agility is crucial for business success, the capacity to implement change smoothly and rapidly can be a significant differentiator.

Finally, Human-Centric Change Management aligns well with broader corporate social-responsibility goals. By prioritizing the well-being and development of employees during times of change, organizations demonstrate a commitment to ethical business practices. This can enhance the company's reputation among stakeholders, including customers, investors, and potential employees.

Call to Action

The benefits of Human-Centric Change Management are comprehensive and transformative. From increased success rates of change initiatives to improved employee engagement, from enhanced organizational resilience to stronger corporate cultures, this approach offers a multitude of advantages. As organizations continue to navigate an increasingly complex and rapidly changing business landscape, adopting a human-centric approach to change management is not just beneficial—it's essential for sustainable success and growth. By recognizing and valuing the human element in organizational transformation, companies can create change that is not only more effective but also more meaningful and enriching for all involved.

As Jurgen Appelo, a pioneer in creative management, says, "The most successful organizations don't just manage change, they lead it by focusing on their most valuable asset—their people."

> So, are you ready to navigate the complexities of organizational change while honoring the human experience at its core?

7

Integrating Agile and Human-Centric Change Management

In today's rapidly evolving business landscape, organizations face the dual challenge of implementing change quickly and ensuring that these changes are embraced and sustained by their workforce. This necessitates a fusion of two powerful methods: Agile, known for its iterative approach and rapid adaptability, and Human-Centric Change Management, which prioritizes the needs and experiences of individuals affected by change. Integrating these approaches creates a dynamic framework that not only accelerates the pace of change but also ensures that people remain at the heart of the transformation journey.

Distinct Yet Complementary Forces in Transformation

Agile practices and Human-Centric Change Management often intersect, leading to confusion about their roles and relationship with each other. While both are crucial components of successful transformation initiatives, it's essential to understand that they are distinct disciplines with unique focuses and methods.

While Agile primarily deals with how work is done, Human-Centric Change Management is concerned with how people adapt to and embrace new ways of working. Agile practices can rapidly introduce new processes or technologies, but without effective change management, these innovative approaches may face resistance or fail to be fully adopted. Human-Centric Change Management provides the tools to address this human element, ensuring that the changes implemented through Agile practices are understood, accepted, and sustained over time.

The key difference lies in their primary focus: Agile is about delivering value through iterative improvement and adaptability, while Human-Centric Change Management is about guiding people through the transition process. Agile asks, "How can we deliver value more effectively?" while Human-Centric Change Management asks, "How can we help people embrace and thrive in this new environment?"

Despite these differences, Agile and Human-Centric Change Management are highly complementary in the context of organizational transformation. Agile's iterative approach allows organizations to introduce changes gradually in manageable increments. This incremental approach often faces less resistance as it makes the change process less overwhelming for employees. Additionally, Agile's emphasis on feedback and continuous improvement provides valuable data, helping to identify areas where additional support or communication may be needed.

So, to repeat, Agile and Human-Centric Change Management are distinct disciplines, and they are both essential components of successful organizational transformation. Agile provides the framework for implementing change quickly and flexibly, while Human-Centric Change Management ensures that these changes are understood, accepted, and internalized by the people within the organization. By recognizing the unique contributions of each approach and integrating them in tandem, organizations can navigate the complex terrain of transformation more effectively.

Shift Happens

The integration process begins with a fundamental shift in how change is conceptualized within the organization. Rather than viewing change as a linear process with a defined start and end point, it is reframed as a continuous, iterative journey. This aligns with Agile's principle of constant improvement while acknowledging the human-centric reality that adaptation is an ongoing process for individuals and teams.

One of the key ways Agile practices support change initiatives is through their emphasis on iterative progress and feedback loops. In most Agile frameworks, work is broken down into small, manageable chunks, with frequent opportunities for review and adjustment. This approach naturally lends itself to change initiatives, allowing organizations to implement them gradually, gather feedback, and tweak things as necessary along the way. This not only makes change more manageable for individuals but also allows for continuous learning and improvement.

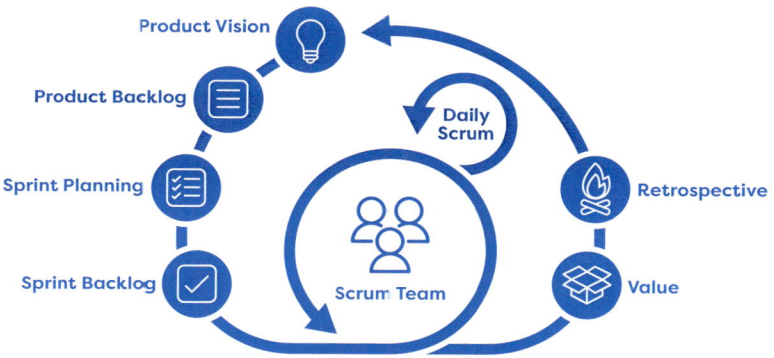

Agile complements the human-centric approach by engaging with employees at every level and encouraging different teams and functions to collaborate with each other rather than work in isolation. This ensures diverse insight and expertise from a wide range of employees so that any changes are informed by and responsive to the needs of those most affected. This collaborative ethos aligns with the human-centric principle of engaging stakeholders at all levels of the organization.

Transparency and open communication, cornerstones of Agile practices, also support effective change management. Reoccurring Agile events create opportunities for ongoing dialogue about the change process, allowing issues to be identified and addressed promptly. This transparency helps build trust and engagement, two critical factors in successful human-centric change initiatives.

Agile events can also be used as opportunities for human-centric change work, such as incorporating change-related discussions into retrospectives. Retrospectives provide space and time to reflect on the current state of affairs and prepare for making any needed adjustments. Applying Agile practices like minimum viable product (MVP) to change initiatives allows for quick wins and iterative improvements, while utilizing Agile's focus on metrics and data helps measure the human impact of transformation using both quantitative and qualitative indicators.

The Agile principle of customer-centricity parallels the human-centric approach to change. Just as Agile teams focus on delivering value to the customer, Human-Centric Change Management emphasizes understanding and addressing the needs of those affected by the change. This shared focus on the end user or stakeholder ensures that change initiatives remain relevant and valuable to those they impact most directly.

Aligning to the Agile Manifesto

The Four Agile Values

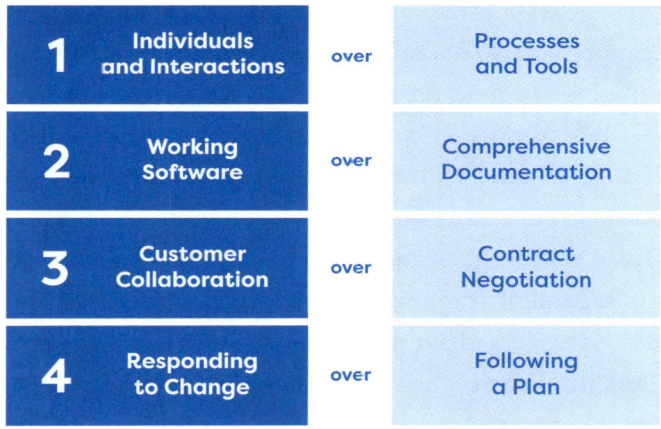

When examining the Agile Manifesto alongside the principles of Human-Centric Change Management, several striking similarities emerge. Both approaches prioritize individuals and interactions over processes and tools, recognizing that human relationships and communication are key drivers of success. They both emphasize responding to change over following a rigid plan, acknowledging the need for flexibility and adaptability in the face of evolving circumstances.

Customer collaboration is valued over contract negotiation in both philosophies, stressing the importance of ongoing engagement with stakeholders throughout the process. Lastly, both Agile and Human-Centric Change Management prioritize working solutions over comprehensive documentation, focusing on practical, tangible progress rather than excessive paperwork.

These parallels demonstrate that Agile and Human-Centric Change Management are not just compatible but mutually reinforcing. By integrating these methods, organizations can create a change management framework that is both structured and flexible, data-driven and emotionally intelligent. This integration allows for rapid experimentation and learning while maintaining a deep focus on the human elements of change.

Successfully blending Agile practices with Human-Centric Change Management requires thoughtful implementation. Leaders must be mindful of potential challenges, such as resistance to the Agile mindset itself or the need to balance Agile's rapid pace with the time required for deep human-centric work. Organizations should strive to educate their workforce about the principles of both, highlighting their complementary nature.

Illustration

In today's fast-paced, volatile business environment, traditional change management approaches often struggle to keep pace. Rigid, waterfall-style methodologies tend to be ineffective in the face of rapidly shifting market conditions, evolving customer needs, and disruptive innovations.

One organization that has found success by blending Agile practices with a human-centric approach to change is Blue Sky Network, a rapidly growing technology firm specializing in enterprise cloud solutions. As the company expanded its product suite and sought to drive deeper client engagement, the leadership team recognized the need for a major internal transformation.

Rather than rolling out a predetermined, top-down change plan, Blue Sky Network embraced an iterative, collaborative approach grounded in the Agile principles. Cross-functional teams were empowered to experiment with new ways of working, test hypotheses, and quickly adapt based on real-time feedback. Regular "sprint reviews" encouraged open dialogue, transparency, and continuous learning.

Importantly, Blue Sky Network placed equal

emphasis on the human side of change, recognizing that sustainable transformation requires more than just process improvements. The company invested heavily in upskilling employees, helping them develop the mindset and skills needed to thrive in an Agile environment. Frequent retrospectives created safe spaces for team members to voice concerns, share lessons learned, and suggest enhancements.

By weaving together Agile practices and the Human-Centric Change Management method, Blue Sky Network was able to navigate its transformation journey with agility and resilience. Rather than imposing a rigid change plan, the company fostered an adaptive, "fail-fast" culture that empowered employees to drive continuous improvement. Frontline teams felt a greater sense of ownership and autonomy, which boosted morale, reduced resistance, and accelerated the pace of change.

The results were impressive. Blue Sky Network was able to rapidly roll out new product features, optimize internal workflows, and deepen its partnerships with clients—all while maintaining high levels of employee engagement and customer satisfaction. The company's revenue skyrocketed, and it established a reputation as an innovative industry leader.

The Blue Sky Network story highlights the power of integrating Agile and Human-Centric Change Management. By embracing an iterative, people-focused approach, the organization was able to navigate uncertainty, manage complexity, and unlock new sources of value. Rather than resisting change, employees became enthusiastic Change Champions, driving the transformation agenda forward with energy and enthusiasm.

In today's dynamic business landscape, the ability to rapidly adapt and evolve is a critical competitive advantage. By blending Agile principles with Human-Centric Change Management, forward-thinking organizations can turn change from a dreaded challenge into an empowering opportunity.

Call to Action

By embracing this human-centric Agile approach to change management, you're not just managing change—you're cultivating an adaptive, resilient organization.

The integration of Agile practices with Human-Centric Change Management represents a powerful evolution in how organizations approach and implement change. It bridges the gap between iterative, flexible changes and a deep understanding of human dynamics, offering a robust framework for navigating the complexities of modern organizational transformation.

By combining Agile's emphasis on adaptability, rapid iteration, and continuous feedback with Human-Centric Change Management's focus on individual experiences, emotions, and motivations, organizations can create change initiatives that are both responsive to shifting external factors and deeply attuned to the needs and capabilities of their workforce.

The synergy of these approaches addresses many of the shortcomings of traditional change management models. It acknowledges the nonlinear nature of change, embracing uncertainty and complexity rather than trying to eliminate them. By breaking down large-scale changes into smaller, manageable increments, this integrated approach reduces overwhelm and resistance, allowing employees to adapt more comfortably to new ways of working.

In addition, integrating Agile with Human-Centric Change Management fosters a culture of continuous improvement and learning. It encourages organizations to view change not as a one-time event but as an ongoing process of evolution and growth. This shift in perspective can lead to more resilient, adaptive organizations.

> So, are you ready to focus on speed, empathy, efficiency, and understanding?

8

Using Kanban to Visualize Change Initiatives

As organizations navigate the turbulent waters of transformation, leaders are increasingly turning to Kanban as a powerful tool for visualizing and managing change initiatives. Rooted in the principles and practices outlined in The Kanban Guide, this collaborative strategy offers a tactical, people-focused approach that can significantly enhance the effectiveness of Human-Centric Change Management efforts. By aligning Kanban's core principles with the tenets of Human-Centric Change Management, organizations can cultivate a more holistic approach to navigating periods of upheaval and uncertainty.

Visualize Everything

At the heart of Kanban lies the principle of visualization—the idea that by making work, processes, and progress visible, teams can gain clarity, promote collaboration, and quickly identify and address bottlenecks. This emphasis on transparency directly supports the Human-Centric Change Management imperative of open communication and trust-building. By breaking down complex change initiatives into a series of actionable steps and making them visually accessible, Kanban helps to alleviate the sense of uncertainty and confusion that often fuels resistance among the workforce.

Kanban's focus on flow is another principle that aligns remarkably well with Human-Centric Change Management. Rather than imposing a rigid, linear change plan, Kanban encourages an iterative, adaptive approach that enables organizations to navigate uncertainty with agility. This flexibility empowers employees to take ownership of the transformation journey, continuously experimenting, learning, and refining their approach based on real-time feedback and evolving circumstances. In so doing, Kanban reinforces the human-centric ethos of shared purpose and collective accountability.

Perhaps most significantly, Kanban's collaborative nature directly supports the core tenets of Human-Centric Change Management. By establishing cross-functional "pull" systems and encouraging active dialogue, the method cultivates a sense of shared ownership and mutual support. Employees are not merely passive recipients of change but rather active participants who can shape and influence the outcome. This people-centric focus helps to unlock new sources of energy, creativity, and resilience—all of which are essential in today's rapidly evolving business landscape.

The Advantage

When implemented thoughtfully and holistically, the fusion of Kanban and Human-Centric Change Management can be a potent force for driving sustainable transformation. By harnessing the power of visual workflow management, leaders can develop a change process that is transparent, adaptable, and deeply aligned with the needs and experiences of the workforce. In the process, they create an environment where people feel empowered, engaged, and invested in the organization's transformation journey.

To effectively integrate Kanban into a Human-Centric Change Management strategy, organizations should consider the following tactical steps:

1. **Establish a Kanban Board:** Create a visual representation of the change process, complete with clearly defined workflow stages, work-in-progress limits, and commitment points.

2. **Manage Flow:** Reduce the number of initiatives the organization and teams must focus on during an incremental time period.

3. **Empower Cross-Functional Teams:** Assemble diverse, collaborative teams that can work together to manage the flow of change initiatives and quickly address any emerging issues or bottlenecks.

4. **Encourage Continuous Improvement:** Implement regular "kaizen" (improvement) events where teams can reflect on their progress, identify

areas for enhancement, and experiment with new approaches.

5. **Foster Open Communication:** Use the Kanban board as a catalyst for ongoing dialogue, providing opportunities for employees to voice their questions, concerns, and ideas.

6. **Cultivate a Change-Ready Mindset:** Invest in training and development programs that help employees develop the skills, behaviors, and mindset needed to thrive in a Kanban-driven, human-centric change environment.

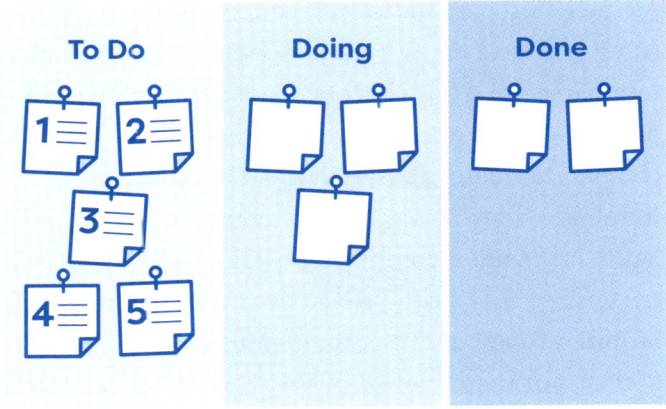

By adopting a tactical, Kanban-infused approach to Human-Centric Change Management, organizations can unlock remarkable levels of agility, resiliency, and innovation—qualities that are essential in today's rapidly evolving business landscape. Through increased transparency, collaborative problem-solving, and a shared sense of ownership, Kanban can help transform change from a daunting challenge into an empowering opportunity.

Illustration

As the healthcare industry faced unprecedented disruption during the COVID pandemic, Coastal Health found itself at a critical crossroads. Antiquated technology systems, siloed workflows, and an increasingly complex regulatory landscape had left the once-dominant provider struggling to keep pace with more agile, innovative competitors. The leadership team recognized that a comprehensive transformation was required to ensure the organization's long-term viability, but they knew that implementing sweeping changes would be no easy feat.

Determined to take a more human-centric approach, the executives at Coastal Health turned to Kanban as a means of visualizing and managing their change initiatives. Rather than rolling out a top-down, prescriptive transformation plan, they empowered cross-functional teams to collaboratively map out the various stages of the change process using a Kanban board.

This visual tool proved to be a game changer. By breaking down the complex change agenda into a series of discrete, actionable steps, the teams gained unprecedented clarity and transparency. Employees across the organization could easily see where their work fit into the bigger picture, fostering an enhanced sense of purpose and ownership.

Crucially, the Kanban board also served as a catalyst for ongoing dialogue and problem-solving. During regular "stand-up" events, team members would gather around the board to discuss progress, identify bottlenecks, and experiment with new approaches. This collaborative, transparent way of working stood in stark contrast to the siloed, directive change management tactics of the past, dramatically reducing resistance and increasing engagement.

As the Coastal Health teams navigated the

transformation journey, they leveraged Kanban's principles of flow and continuous improvement to great effect. Rather than adhering rigidly to a predetermined plan, they were empowered to continuously adapt and refine their methods based on real-time feedback and evolving business needs. Work-in-progress limits and "pull" systems helped to optimize the pace of change, preventing teams from becoming overwhelmed or bogged down.

The results were nothing short of remarkable. By harnessing the power of Kanban to visualize and streamline their change initiatives, Coastal Health was able to rapidly overhaul its technology infrastructure, realign its workforce, and enhance its patient-centric service offerings. Productivity soared as employees channeled their energy into productive problem-solving rather than passive resistance. Morale and retention rates skyrocketed as people felt deeply invested in the organization's transformation agenda.

Perhaps most significantly, Coastal Health's Kanban-driven, human-centric approach to change enabled the organization to navigate a turbulent period for the industry with remarkable agility and resilience. Rather than succumbing to the disruptive forces of the market, the company emerged as a leaner, more innovative healthcare leader—a testament to the power of blending Kanban's tactical principles with a steadfast commitment to empowering and engaging the workforce.

This powerful narrative underscores the transformative potential of Kanban when applied through the lens of Human-Centric Change Management. By providing a visual, collaborative framework for driving organizational transformation, Kanban can help leaders in the healthcare industry overcome the common pitfalls of change initiatives by streamlining processes, fostering transparency, and unleashing the creative potential of their most valuable asset: their people.

Call to Action

In a period of unprecedented change and disruption in the business environment, organizations that can effectively navigate the human dimensions of transformation will be best positioned to thrive. By integrating Kanban's principles and practices into their change management strategies, leaders can develop a more holistic, people-centric approach that unlocks the full potential of their workforce. Ultimately, the fusion of Kanban and Human-Centric Change Management represents a powerful pathway for organizations seeking to create a brighter, more adaptable future.

> **So, are you ready to visualize and prioritize?**

9

The Art of Communication

Communication serves as the lifeblood of any change initiative, flowing through every level of the organization and carrying with it the power to inform, inspire, and unite. In the context of Human-Centric Change Management, communication takes on an even more profound significance. It's not just about disseminating information; it's about creating a shared understanding, fostering dialogue, and building trust.

When an organization embarks on a change journey, employees naturally seek answers to a myriad of questions: Why is this change necessary? How will it affect me? What's expected of me? Clear, consistent, and empathetic communication addresses these concerns, helping to alleviate anxiety and resistance. It provides a narrative that connects the change to the organization's broader vision and each individual's role within it.

Communication in Human-Centric Change Management goes beyond top-down messaging. It creates channels for two-way dialogue, encouraging feedback, questions, and ideas from all levels of the organization. This inclusive approach not only improves the quality of the change initiative by incorporating diverse perspectives but also increases buy-in and ownership among employees.

The Risks of Poor Communication

When communication falters during a change process, the consequences can be severe and far-reaching. Poor communication leaves a vacuum that is often filled with rumors, misinformation, and speculation. This can lead to increased anxiety among employees, fostering a climate of distrust and resistance. Without clear information, individuals may feel threatened by the change, leading to decreased productivity and engagement.

Furthermore, inadequate communication can result in misalignment between various parts of the organization. Teams may work at cross-purposes, leading to inefficiencies and frustration. The lack of a unified message can cause confusion about priorities and expectations, potentially derailing the change initiative entirely.

In the worst cases, poor communication during change can lead to a loss of talent. When employees feel left in the dark or undervalued, they may seek opportunities elsewhere, taking with them valuable skills and institutional knowledge. This brain drain can significantly impact the organization's ability to implement and sustain change effectively.

The Benefits of Clear and Frequent Communication

On the flip side, when communication is clear, frequent, and aligned with Human-Centric Change Management principles, the benefits are substantial. Primarily, this creates a sense of transparency and openness, which builds trust between leadership and employees. Such trust is crucial for overcoming the natural resistance to change.

Clear communication helps to create a shared vision of the future state. When employees understand not just what is changing but why it's changing and how it connects to the organization's goals, they're more likely to support and actively contribute to the change effort. This shared vision acts as a North Star, guiding decisions and actions throughout the change process.

Frequent communication keeps the change initiative at the forefront of everyone's mind, maintaining momentum and enthusiasm. It provides opportunities to celebrate small wins along the way, reinforcing positive behaviors and demonstrating progress. This ongoing dialogue also allows for course corrections as needed, ensuring the change effort remains responsive to evolving circumstances and feedback.

Communication in Human-Centric Change Management empowers employees. By providing channels for feedback and actively listening to concerns and ideas, leaders tap into the collective intelligence of their workforce. This not only improves the quality of the change initiative but also increases employee engagement and ownership of the process.

Clear and frequent communication also helps to manage expectations realistically. By openly discussing challenges as well as opportunities, leadership can prepare their workforce for the ups and downs of the change journey. This honesty fosters resilience and adaptability, crucial qualities in today's fast-paced business environment.

Illustration

When it comes to navigating organizational change, effective communication is not merely a "nice-to-have"—it is an absolute imperative. Time and again, poorly executed or infrequent communication has been the downfall of well-intentioned change initiatives, undermining employee buy-in, eroding trust, and ultimately derailing transformation efforts.

One such cautionary tale can be found at Pharmicus, a once-thriving manufacturer of generic drug products. Facing increasing global competition and pricing pressures, Pharmicus's leadership team determined that a comprehensive overhaul of the company's operations and business model was required to remain viable. They developed an ambitious transformation plan that touched nearly every aspect of the organization, from supply chain optimization to workforce realignment.

However, from the outset, Pharmicus's communication efforts fell woefully short. Executives provided sporadic updates, often using technical jargon and financial metrics that left frontline employees confused and disconnected. When the inevitable challenges and setbacks arose, the leadership team hunkered down, choosing to "wait out the storm" rather than proactively addressing concerns. Rumors and misinformation quickly proliferated, fueling widespread anxiety and resentment among the workforce.

Unsurprisingly, the change initiative stalled. With morale plummeting and trust in short supply, employees grew increasingly resistant, finding creative ways to undermine the new processes and systems. The transformation plan quickly descended into chaos, and Pharmicus found itself hemorrhaging top talent as people sought more stable employment opportunities.

Recognizing the need for a course correction, Pharmicus's new CEO made communication the centerpiece of the company's renewed change efforts. She instituted a robust, multifaceted communication strategy that emphasized clarity, transparency, and consistency.

Regular town hall meetings provided a forum for honest dialogue, allowing employees to voice their questions and concerns directly to leadership. The CEO herself conducted frequent "fireside chats," sharing personal insights and updates in an approachable, relatable manner. Detailed progress reports were distributed via multiple channels, ensuring that all staff members remained informed and aligned. Importantly, the communication efforts did not end once the initial change plan was rolled out—they continued uninterrupted throughout the transformation journey, adapting to emerging needs and evolving circumstances.

The impact was profound. As employees began to feel heard, understood, and valued, resistance gave way to cautious optimism. People channeled their energy into productive problem-solving rather than passive-aggressive undermining. The pace of change accelerated as frontline teams collaborated actively to identify and implement continuous improvements.

Ultimately, Pharmicus's renewed focus on communication proved to be a game changer, transforming the company's change initiative from a crisis into a success story. By prioritizing clarity, consistency, and openness, the leadership team was able to build the trust and engagement necessary to navigate the rough terrain of organizational transformation.

Effective communication is the lifeblood of successful change management. When done well, it can inspire, empower, and unite people around a shared vision. But when communication falters, change initiatives are doomed to flounder. For organizations seeking to drive sustainable transformation, mastering the art of communication must be a top priority.

Call to Action

Communication is not just a component of Human-Centric Change Management; it is the very fabric that holds the process together. When executed thoughtfully and consistently, it transforms change from a top-down directive to a collaborative journey. By prioritizing clear, frequent, and empathetic communication, organizations can navigate the complexities of change while honoring the human experience at its core. In doing so, they not only increase the likelihood of successful change implementation but also build a more engaged, resilient, and united workforce capable of thriving in an ever-evolving landscape.

> So, are you ready to provide clear, consistent, and continuous communication?

10

Reimagining Change Management Roles

In the realm of traditional change management, several key roles have long been established to guide organizations through periods of transition. These roles, while effective, are now undergoing a transformation as the field shifts toward a more human-centric approach.

Leaning into our Agile mindset, remember that roles are not equivalent or interchangeable with titles. A role typically describes the actual duties and functions an individual performs, while a title is often a more formal designation that may not always accurately reflect day-to-day activities. This distinction matters because roles can evolve over time, adapting to organizational needs, whereas titles tend to be more static and may not keep pace with changes in responsibilities.

In Human-Centric Change Management, we're focused on the roles, not the titles.

Shifting from Traditional to Human-Centric Roles

The Change Sponsor, typically a senior executive, has traditionally been responsible for initiating and supporting change initiatives from the top down. Their role has been to provide resources, remove obstacles, and communicate the importance of change to the organization. In the human-centric approach, the Change Sponsor becomes more of a Change Champion, actively engaging with employees at all levels to understand their perspectives and concerns. They focus on creating a psychologically safe environment where individuals feel comfortable expressing their thoughts and emotions about the change process.

Change Managers have conventionally been tasked with planning and executing change strategies. They've focused on developing timelines, managing resources, and tracking progress. Within Human-Centric Change Management, Change Managers evolve into Change Facilitators. While still overseeing the practical aspects of transformation, they place greater emphasis on fostering dialogue, building relationships, and nurturing a culture of continuous learning and adaptation. They become skilled in emotional intelligence and conflict resolution, recognizing that successful change is as much about managing emotions as it is about managing activities.

Change Agents, traditionally recruited from various departments to champion initiatives within their teams, have often been selected based on their influence and position within the organization. In the human-centric approach, these individuals become Change Advocates. Their selection is based not only on their position but also on their empathy, listening skills, and ability to connect with colleagues on a personal level. They are trained to recognize and address the human impact of change, providing support and guidance to their peers throughout the transition process.

The role of communications specialists in traditional change management has been to craft and disseminate messages about the change initiative. From a human-centric perspective, they transform into Engagement Catalysts. Their focus shifts from one-way communication to fostering two-way dialogue and creating opportunities for meaningful employee participation in the change process. They develop platforms for story-sharing, encourage feedback loops, and help create a narrative that resonates with the individual experiences of those affected by the change.

Training and development professionals have typically concentrated on equipping employees with the skills and knowledge needed to adapt to new systems or processes. Looking at training and development through the human-centric lens, they become Learning Experience Designers. Their role expands to include not only technical training but also the development of emotional resilience, adaptability, and change readiness. They create personalized learning journeys that acknowledge the diverse needs and learning styles of individuals within the organization.

Human resources professionals, often involved in managing the people-related aspects of change, evolve through this model from their traditional role into Talent Experience Architects. In Human-Centric Change Management, they focus on aligning the change initiative with employee well-being, career aspirations, and personal growth. They work to ensure that the change process enhances rather than diminishes employee engagement and satisfaction.

Illustration

Traditionally, change management has been the domain of a specialized team of experts—typically consultants or internal specialists tasked with driving the technical aspects of transformation initiatives. Their focus is on meticulously planning and executing the sequence of activities, tracking milestones, and ensuring adherence to the change management methodology.

While this traditional approach has its merits, it often falls short when it comes to addressing the human side of change. By relegating change management to a siloed function, organizations risk creating a disconnect between the technical imperatives and the lived experiences of frontline employees. In this model, the change process can feel disjointed, impersonal, and disconnected from the day-to-day realities of the workforce.

One organization that has found success by reimagining the change management role is Fusion.io, a regional IT solutions provider. Rather than relying on a centralized change management team, Fusion.io has empowered Change Champions—employees from across the organization who volunteer to serve as ambassadors and advocates for the company's transformation agenda.

These Change Champions come from diverse backgrounds and functional areas, bringing a rich tapestry of experiences, perspectives, and relationships to the table. They are not change management experts per se but rather passionate individuals who are eager to shepherd their colleagues through periods of upheaval and uncertainty.

The Change Champions play a vital role in bridging the gap between leadership directives and the frontline workforce. They serve as conduits for communication, translating strategic objectives into actionable, contextual terms. They also provide a critical feedback loop, surfacing employee concerns, ideas, and pain points that the central change management team may have missed.

Importantly, these Change Champions are empowered to take ownership of the transformation process within their respective domains. They are given the autonomy and resources to experiment with new approaches, troubleshoot challenges, and drive continuous improvement. Regular "office hours" and team-based "change check-ins" allow them to offer hands-on support and coaching to their colleagues.

The results speak for themselves. By decentralizing change management and tapping into the collective energy and creativity of the workforce, Fusion.io has achieved remarkable success in driving sustainable transformation. Employees feel heard, supported, and invested in amid the change process, resulting in higher levels of engagement, collaboration, and resilience.

The Change Champion model has had a powerful ripple effect, inspiring a broader cultural shift toward adaptability and continuous improvement. As people see their colleagues stepping up to champion change, they are motivated to develop their own change management capabilities, expanding the pool of internal change leaders.

Fusion.io demonstrates the value of reimagining the role of change management through a more human-centric lens. By empowering frontline employees to serve as change agents, organizations can unlock new sources of energy, creativity, and ownership—ultimately accelerating the pace of transformation and enhancing the likelihood of long-term success.

Call to Action

As we reimagine roles in change management, it becomes clear that the shift from traditional to human-centric approaches is not merely a trend but a necessity in today's complex and rapidly changing organizational landscape. Traditional roles, while foundational, often prioritized processes over people, potentially overlooking the human experience that is central to successful change.

By reimagining these roles through a human-centric lens, organizations can create a more inclusive, empathetic, and effective approach to change. This shift acknowledges that change is not just about implementing new strategies or technologies but also about guiding people through personal and professional transformations. It recognizes that the success of any change initiative ultimately depends on the willingness and ability of individuals to embrace and drive that change.

The evolution of these roles represents a fundamental shift in how organizations approach change—moving from a top-down, process-first model to one that places human experiences, emotions, and relationships at its core. As we continue to navigate an increasingly complex and interconnected world, this human-centric approach to change management will be essential in building resilient, adaptive, and thriving organizations.

> So, are you ready to reimagine your change management roles?

11

Leading Human-Centric Change Management

As a leader, you've likely encountered your fair share of change initiatives. You've seen firsthand how these efforts can falter when they fail to account for the most crucial element of any organization: its people. Human-Centric Change Management requires a shift in leadership style, transforming the way you approach and implement change.

Leading People and Change

You begin by recognizing that change is not merely a matter of processes and systems but a deeply human experience. Your employees are not cogs in a machine but individuals with hopes, fears, and unique perspectives. By placing their needs and experiences at the heart of your change strategy, you set the stage for more successful and sustainable transformations.

Your journey starts with communication. You understand that transparency is key to building trust and reducing resistance. As you craft your change narrative, you focus on clarity and honesty. You explain the reasons behind the change, painting a vivid picture of the desired future state. But you don't stop there. You acknowledge the challenges that lie ahead and the potential impact on your team. By doing so, you demonstrate respect for your employees' intelligence and emotional maturity.

Next, you turn your attention to involvement. You recognize that change imposed from above rarely takes root. Instead, you seek to cocreate the change with your team. You organize workshops and feedback sessions, actively soliciting ideas and concerns from all levels of the organization. You listen—truly listen—to what your people have to say. Their insights often surprise you, revealing blind spots in your initial plans and opening new possibilities.

As you move forward, empathy remains at the forefront of your mind. You understand that change can be unsettling, even frightening, for many. You encourage your management team to practice active listening and to respond with compassion to employees' concerns. You create safe spaces for people to express their anxieties without fear of judgment. By acknowledging and validating these emotions, you help your team move through them more quickly and effectively.

You also recognize that change is not a one-size-fits-all process. You take the time to understand the varying needs and capacities of different individuals and teams within your organization. Some may embrace change eagerly, while others require more time and support. You tailor your approach accordingly, providing additional resources and guidance where needed.

Throughout the change process, you ensure that your team has access to the training, tools, and support they need to navigate the transition successfully. You frame this as an opportunity for growth and development, helping your employees see how the change can enhance their skills and advance their careers.

You also understand the power of culture in driving change. You work to foster an environment that embraces learning, experimentation, and continuous improvement. You encourage calculated risk-taking and view setbacks as valuable learning opportunities. By doing so, you help your team become more adaptable and resilient in the face of change.

As changes are made, you pay close attention to progress and milestones. You celebrate small wins along the way, recognizing the efforts of individuals and teams who are leading the charge. These celebrations serve dual purposes: they boost morale and motivation while also demonstrating the positive impact of the changes being implemented.

Throughout this process, you lead by example. You embody the behaviors and attitudes you wish to see in your organization. If the change requires new skills or ways of working, you're the first to engage in learning and development. Your actions speak louder than words, inspiring your team to follow suit.

You also identify and empower Change Champions within your organization. These are individuals who naturally embrace the change and have the respect of their peers. You provide them with additional support and resources, enabling them to become Change Advocates and mentors for others in their teams or departments.

As you progress, you maintain a flexible mindset. You continuously monitor the impact of your change initiatives, seeking feedback from all levels of the organization. You're not afraid to adjust your strategies based on this input. You understand that human-centric change is an iterative process, requiring constant refinement and adaptation.

Effective Leadership Characteristics

By embracing Human-Centric Change Management, you transform not just your organization but also your own leadership style. You become more than a manager of processes; you become a steward of your people's growth and well-being. As you witness the positive impact of this approach—increased engagement, smoother transitions, and more sustainable changes—you realize that putting humans at the center of change isn't just the right thing to do. It's the smart thing to do.

The most effective leaders in this context embody the following characteristics:

- **Emotional Intelligence:** Be adept at recognizing and managing your own emotions and those of others.

- **Adaptive Leadership:** Be comfortable with uncertainty and skilled at helping others learn and adapt.

- **Servant Leadership:** Your focus should be on empowering and supporting others through change.

- **Systems Thinking:** Understand the interconnections within your organization and how change ripples through the system.

- **Growth Mindset:** Leaders need to model and foster a growth mindset, viewing challenges as opportunities for learning and development.

- **Authenticity and Vulnerability:** Authentic leaders who are willing to show vulnerability can create psychological safety, essential for navigating change.

- **Coaching Ability:** Leaders need to be skilled coaches, able to ask powerful questions and support others in finding their own solutions.

- **Cultural Intelligence:** In our globalized world, leaders need cultural intelligence (CQ). This involves adapting your approach to change across diverse cultural contexts.

Putting People First

Leaders who introduce Human-Centric Change Management into their organizations should adopt a holistic and empathetic approach. They can begin by fostering a culture of openness and psychological safety, where employees feel comfortable expressing their thoughts and concerns about change. Leaders should actively listen to their team members, seeking to understand the human impact of organizational transitions.

They can act as role models by showing vulnerability when sharing their own experiences with change, demonstrating that it's normal to feel uncertain or apprehensive. Investing in training programs that focus on emotional intelligence and resilience can equip both leaders and employees with the skills needed to navigate change effectively. Leaders should communicate clearly, explaining the reasons for changes and involving employees in the decision-making process where possible.

By consistently being mindful of people's feelings during change, leaders can gradually shift the organizational mindset toward a more human-centric approach. This transition requires patience and persistence, as it often involves challenging long-held beliefs about how change should be managed.

Ultimately, leaders should strive to create an environment where change is seen not just as a business necessity but as an opportunity for personal and collective growth.

A Sustainable Approach

To introduce Human-Centric Change Management into an organization, leaders should consider the following approaches:

Prioritize employee involvement:

- Engage employees at all levels in the change process.
- Seek input and feedback regularly.
- Create channels for open communication.

Focus on empathy and emotional intelligence:

- Understand and address employees' concerns and fears.
- Provide emotional support throughout the transition.
- Train managers in emotional intelligence skills.

Tailor communication strategies:

- Develop clear, transparent messaging about the change.
- Use multiple communication channels to reach all employees.
- Provide context and rationale for the changes.

Invest in training and development:

- Offer skill-building opportunities to support the change.
- Provide resources for continuous learning.
- Ensure employees feel equipped to manage new responsibilities.

Create a supportive culture:

- Foster an environment that embraces change and innovation.
- Encourage experimentation and learning from failures.
- Recognize and reward adaptability.

Lead by example:

- Demonstrate commitment to the change process.
- Model desired behaviors and attitudes.
- Be open about personal challenges and growth.

Implement change gradually:

- Break down substantial changes into smaller, manageable steps.
- Allow time for adjustment between phases.
- Be flexible and willing to adjust the plan based on feedback.

Measure and celebrate progress:

- Define clear metrics for success.
- Regularly assess and communicate progress.
- Celebrate milestones and achievements.

Provide individualized support:

- Recognize that employees may adapt at different speeds.
- Offer personalized coaching or mentoring.
- Address individual concerns and needs.

Establish a change management team:

- Create a dedicated group to oversee the change process.
- Include representatives from various departments and levels.
- Empower this team to make decisions and drive the initiative.

Illustration

For many seasoned leaders, navigating organizational change has become an all-too-familiar challenge. Time and again, they have dutifully crafted comprehensive transformation strategies, meticulously tracked key performance indicators, and rigorously enforced new policies and processes only to see these well-intentioned efforts fall short, bogged down by entrenched resistance, employee disengagement, and a general lack of sustained momentum.

Such was the case at Pinnacle Financial, a longstanding financial services provider that found itself in the throes of a major digital transformation.

Recognizing the need to modernize its technology infrastructure, streamline operations, and enhance its customer experience, the executive team developed an ambitious multiyear plan to overhaul the company's core systems and realign the workforce.

Employing a traditional, top-down approach to change management, the leaders at Pinnacle relied heavily on directive communication, performance management systems, and incremental targets to drive the transformation agenda forward. They placed their faith in the power of process and structure, believing that if they could just get the "moving parts" aligned, the rest would naturally fall into place.

However, this myopic focus on the technical aspects of change soon began to unravel. Frontline employees grew increasingly disenchanted, perceiving the new initiatives as disconnected from their day-to-day realities and lacking in genuine empathy for their needs and concerns. Productivity plummeted as people actively resisted the changes, finding creative ways to undermine the new systems and processes. Engagement substantially decreased, creating a culture of quiet quitting, and Pinnacle began hemorrhaging top talent as people sought more fulfilling opportunities elsewhere.

Recognizing that their conventional leadership approach was no longer sufficient, the Pinnacle executives made the bold decision to fundamentally rethink their change management strategy. They adopted a more human-centric mindset, placing the needs, fears, and aspirations of their workforce at the forefront of the transformation efforts.

This shift manifested in a variety of ways. The leaders became more visible and accessible, regularly engaging with employees through town halls, one-on-one conversations, and informal check-ins. They actively solicited feedback, creating safe spaces for people to voice their concerns and ideas without fear of repercussions. Crucially, they demonstrated a genuine willingness to adapt and evolve the change plan based on the insights gleaned from these interactions.

The leadership team also invested heavily in upskilling and empowering their people. Robust training programs helped employees develop the mindset and skills needed to thrive in a rapidly changing environment. Cross-functional "change champion" networks were established, providing frontline staff with the support, resources, and autonomy necessary to drive continuous improvement within their domains.

The results were transformative. As employees began to feel heard, supported, and valued, resistance gradually gave way to enthusiasm and collaboration. People channeled their energy into problem-solving rather than passive-aggressive undermining, readily embracing the new technologies and workflows. Productivity soared, and Pinnacle's reputation as an employer of choice was restored, enabling the company to attract and retain top talent.

Ultimately, Pinnacle's shift toward human-centric leadership proved to be the linchpin of its successful transformation. By placing people at the heart of the change agenda, the leaders were able to unlock remarkable levels of agility, resilience, and innovation—qualities that proved essential in navigating the unpredictable, fast-paced financial services landscape.

The ability to lead change through a human-centric lens is not just a "nice-to-have"; it is a strategic imperative. Organizations that empower their leaders to prioritize the needs and experiences of their workforce will be best positioned to drive sustainable transformation and unlock new sources of competitive advantage.

Call to Action

Leading Human-Centric Change Management represents a paradigm shift in how organizations navigate transitions and transformations. This approach recognizes that at the heart of every change initiative are people—with their hopes, fears, aspirations, and unique perspectives. As leaders embrace this human-centric philosophy, they pave the way for more sustainable and meaningful change within their organizations.

The journey toward Human-Centric Change Management is not without its challenges. It requires leaders to cultivate new skills, challenge long-held assumptions, and often, transform their own leadership styles. However, the rewards of this approach are substantial. By placing people at the center of change efforts, organizations can tap into the collective wisdom, creativity, and resilience of their workforce, leading to more innovative solutions and smoother transitions.

Human-Centric Change Management fosters a culture of trust, empathy, and continuous learning. It creates an environment where change is not feared but embraced as an opportunity for growth and development. This shift in perspective can have far-reaching effects, enhancing employee engagement, improving organizational agility, and ultimately driving better business outcomes.

As we move forward in an increasingly complex and rapidly evolving business landscape, the ability to lead change with a human-centric focus will become a critical competency for leaders across all industries. Those who master this approach will be better equipped to guide their organizations through the challenges of the future, creating workplaces that are not only more adaptive and resilient but also more fulfilling and purpose-driven for all who are part of them.

The transition to Human-Centric Change Management is more than just a change in processes or methodologies; it's a fundamental reimagining of the relationship between organizations and the people within them. By committing to this approach, leaders can unlock the full potential of their teams, navigate change with greater ease and effectiveness, and build organizations that are truly fit for the future. As we close this chapter, we open the door to a new era of change management—one that puts humans first and, in doing so, paves the way for more successful, sustainable, and meaningful organizational transformations.

> So, are you ready to lead the change you need within your organization?

12

Taking the First Step

As organizations navigate today's business environment, the imperative to embrace a more human-centric approach to change management has never been clearer. Time and again, leaders have witnessed the limitations of traditional, top-down methodologies—approaches that often fail to adequately address the complex human dynamics that can make or break transformation efforts. So a growing number of forward-thinking organizations have begun to prioritize the needs, fears, and aspirations of their workforce, empowering their people to serve as active partners in driving sustainable change.

Yet, for many leaders, the prospect of transitioning to Human-Centric Change Management can feel daunting. Where does one even begin? How can the lofty principles of employee engagement, transparency, and adaptability be translated into tangible, actionable strategies? And perhaps most importantly, how can organizations ensure that this human-centered mindset becomes deeply embedded in their cultural fabric, rather than proving a fleeting fad?

Dr. Sidky provides a great perspective on this challenge: "The journey toward Human-Centric Change Management begins not with grand strategies or complex frameworks, but with a fundamental shift in mindset. Leaders must first recognize that their people are not simply resources to be managed, but partners to be engaged and empowered in the change process."

Where Is the Starting Line?

The first critical step for leaders embarking on this journey is to cultivate a deep, genuine understanding of their workforce. This means going beyond superficial metrics and surveys to truly listen to the lived experiences, pain points, and aspirations of frontline employees. What are the key drivers of resistance and disengagement? Where do people feel most empowered and supported? By taking the time to engage in open, empathetic dialogue, leaders can uncover invaluable insights that will shape the design and implementation of their human-centric change initiatives.

Armed with this enhanced employee-centric perspective, leaders must then work to realign their change management practices to better serve the needs of the workforce. This may involve rethinking traditional communication channels, revamping training and development programs, or even reconsidering the organizational structures and decision-making processes that govern transformation efforts. Importantly, this is not a one-time exercise but rather an ongoing process of continuous learning and adaptation.

Equally critical is the need for leaders to model the behaviors and mindsets they wish to cultivate across the organization. By visibly championing human-centric principles, proactively addressing resistance, and actively soliciting feedback, executives can signal the importance of this strategic shift and inspire their teams to embrace it with enthusiasm and commitment. Furthermore, the establishment of cross-functional Change Champion networks can help to amplify this people-focused ethos, empowering frontline employees to serve as ambassadors and advocates for the transformation agenda.

Ultimately, the true test of a Human-Centric Change Management strategy lies in the extent to which it becomes embedded in the organization's cultural DNA. Rather than existing as a siloed initiative or a temporary fad, this people-first approach must become a core tenet of how the company operates—informing everything from talent management to performance evaluation to strategic planning. By weaving these principles into the very fabric of the organization, leaders can ensure that their workforce remains agile, engaged, and resilient in the face of ongoing change and disruption.

Illustration

In the bustling corridors of Nexus Technologies, a midsize software company, CEO Sarah Chen found herself at a crossroads. The rapidly evolving tech landscape demanded swift adaptation, yet previous attempts at organizational change had fallen flat, leaving employees disengaged and resistant.

Determined to chart a new course, Sarah decided to embrace a human-centric approach to change management. Her journey provides a compelling illustration of the crucial first steps leaders must take when embarking on this transformative path.

Step 1: Self-Reflection and Mindset Shift

Sarah's first move was not to draft a new strategy or convene her executive team. Instead, she carved out time for deep self-reflection. She realized that to lead human-centric change, she needed to first examine her own assumptions and biases about change management. Sarah acknowledged that her previous top-down approach had inadvertently marginalized employee perspectives. This honest self-assessment laid the groundwork for a fundamental shift in her leadership mindset.

Step 2: Listening and Learning

Armed with this new perspective, Sarah launched a company-wide "listening tour." She scheduled informal coffee chats with employees across all levels and departments, asking open-ended questions about their experiences, frustrations, and ideas for improvement. Sarah made it clear that these were not performance reviews but genuine attempts to understand the workforce's needs and aspirations.

Step 3: Creating Psychological Safety

Recognizing that open dialogue requires trust, Sarah took steps to foster psychological safety within the organization. She publicly acknowledged past missteps in change initiatives and shared her own vulnerabilities and learning journey. This demonstration of humility and transparency began to break down barriers and encourage more honest communication throughout Nexus.

Step 4: Empowering Change Champions

Rather than assembling a traditional change management team, Sarah identified and empowered a diverse group of Change Champions from various levels and departments. These individuals were passionate about driving positive change and had strong connections within their teams. Sarah provided them with resources, training, and a direct line of communication to leadership, enabling them to become catalysts for grassroots change efforts.

Step 5: Collaborative Visioning

Instead of presenting a predetermined vision for change, Sarah facilitated a series of collaborative workshops where employees from all corners of the organization contributed to shaping Nexus's future direction. This inclusive process not only yielded innovative ideas but also fostered a sense of ownership and commitment to the change journey ahead.

Step 6: Embracing Experimentation

Sarah introduced the concept of "change experiments"—small-scale, low-risk initiatives designed to test new approaches and gather real-world feedback. Teams were encouraged to propose and lead these experiments, with the understanding that failure was acceptable as long as valuable lessons were learned and shared.

Step 7: Realigning Systems and Processes

Recognizing that sustainable change requires supportive structures, Sarah initiated a review of Nexus's performance management, reward systems, and decision-making processes. She worked with HR and team leaders to ensure these systems aligned with and reinforced the principles of human-centric change.

As these steps unfolded, a palpable shift began to occur at Nexus Technologies. Employees who had once viewed change with skepticism now approached it with cautious optimism. The energy in team meetings was noticeably more positive and collaborative.

While challenges remained, Sarah had successfully laid the groundwork for a more resilient, adaptive, and human-centric approach to change.

The first steps in Human-Centric Change Management are not about grand strategies or immediate overhauls. Instead, they focus on shifting mindsets, building trust, and creating the conditions for genuine engagement and collaboration. By following Sarah's example, leaders can begin to transform their organizations from the inside out, one human-centered step at a time.

Call to Action

The transition to a more human-centric approach to change management is not a simple switch to be flipped but rather a journey of continuous learning and evolution.

Leaders that prioritize the human element of change will be best positioned to thrive amid any approaching turbulent waters. By recognizing employees as true partners in the change process, leaders can unlock unprecedented levels of creativity, resilience, and adaptability—qualities that are essential for long-term success in today's dynamic environment.

The path forward may not always be clear or easy, but by committing to these human-centric principles and taking concrete steps to implement them, leaders can create organizations that are not only more successful but also more fulfilling and inspiring places to work. In doing so, they pave the way for a new era of change management—one that harnesses the full potential of their most valuable asset: their people.

> So, are you ready to look beyond the edge and take the first step?

13

Conclusion

The path to successful organizational transformation lies not in rigid processes or impersonal strategies but in the hearts and minds of the very people who make up our companies. The human approach to change recognizes that behind every spreadsheet, every workflow, and every bottom line, there are individuals with hopes, fears, and unique perspectives.

Throughout this journey, we've seen how acknowledging and embracing the human element can turn potential resistance into powerful momentum. By focusing on empathy, communication, and individual growth, leaders can create an environment where change is not just accepted but enthusiastically embraced. We've learned that when people feel valued, heard, and supported, they become the driving force behind lasting transformation.

CONCLUSION

The future of change management is undoubtedly human-centric. As technology continues to advance and the pace of change accelerates, the need for a compassionate, people-first approach becomes even more critical. Organizations that recognize this will not only navigate changes more smoothly but will also cultivate a resilient, adaptable workforce ready to face future challenges.

Human-Centric Change Management is more than just a methodology; it's a philosophy that respects the inherent dignity and potential of every individual within an organization. It reminds us that at the core of every successful change initiative are people—their creativity, their commitment, and their collective power to shape the future.

As we move forward, let us carry this understanding with us. Let it inform our decisions, guide our actions, and inspire our leadership. For in embracing the human side of change, we don't just transform our organizations—we elevate the human experience of work itself, creating environments where both people and businesses can truly flourish.

CONCLUSION

So, risk-takers and change-makers, are you ready? Let's go!

BIBLIOGRAPHY

Armenakis, A. A., & Harris, S. G. (2009). "Reflections: Our Journey in Organizational Change Research and Practice." *Journal of Change Management*, 9(2), 127–142.

Beck, K., Beedle, M., van Bennekum, A., Cockburn, A., Cunningham, W., Fowler, M., . . . & Thomas, D. (2001). Manifesto for Agile Software Development. Agile Alliance.

Bridges, W. (2009). *Managing Transitions: Making the Most of Change*. Da Capo Press.

Brown, T. (2009). *Change by Design: How Design Thinking Transforms Organizations and Inspires Innovation*. HarperBusiness.

Cameron, E., & Green, M. (2019). *Making Sense of Change Management: A Complete Guide to the Models, Tools and Techniques of Organizational Change*. Kogan Page Publishers.

Choi, M., & Ruona, W. E. (2011). "Individual Readiness for Organizational Change and Its Implications for Human Resource and Organization Development." *Human Resource Development Review*, 10(1), 46–73.

Cohn, M. (2010). Succeeding with Agile: Software Development Using Scrum. Addison-Wesley Professional.

Haidt, J. (2006). *The Happiness Hypothesis: Finding Modern Truth in Ancient Wisdom*. Basic Books.

Heath, C., & Heath, D. (2010). *Switch: How to Change Things When Change Is Hard*. Crown Business.

Heath, C., & Heath, D. (2007). *Made to Stick: Why Some Ideas Survive and Others Die*. Random House.

Hiatt, J. M. (2006). *ADKAR: A Model for Change in Business, Government and Our Community*. Prosci Learning Center Publications.

Kotter, J. P. (2012). *Leading Change*. Harvard Business Review Press.

Kübler-Ross, E. (1969). *On Death and Dying*. Macmillan.

Lewin, K. (1947). Frontiers in Group Dynamics: Concept, Method and Reality in Social Science; Social Equilibria and Social Change. *Human Relations*, 1(1), 5–41.

Prosci Inc. (2018). *Best Practices in Change Management*. Prosci Inc.

Rogers, E. M. (2003). *Diffusion of Innovations* (5th ed.). Free Press.

Schein, E. H. (2010). *Organizational Culture and Leadership* (4th ed.). Jossey-Bass.

Senge, P. M. (2006). *The Fifth Discipline: The Art & Practice of the Learning Organization*. Crown Business.

Sidky, A. (2020). *The Journey to Enterprise Agility: Systems Thinking and Organizational Legacy*. Addison-Wesley Professional.

Sutherland, J., & Schwaber, K. (2017). The Scrum Guide: The Definitive Guide to Scrum: The Rules of the Game. Scrum.org.

ABOUT THE AUTHOR

Elisabeth White is a distinguished thought leader and transformation expert who brings more than fifteen years of experience in driving organizational excellence through human-centric approaches. As cofounder and CEO of Cornerstone Agility Inc., she has established herself as a trusted advisor to senior executives and diverse professional teams across the globe.

Drawing inspiration from Winston Churchill's wisdom that "success is not final, failure is not fatal: it is the courage to continue that counts," Elisabeth has built her career on helping organizations navigate complex transformations with resilience and purpose. Her expertise spans Human-Centric Change Management, Lean Portfolio Management, and leadership coaching, making her a sought-after speaker and consultant in the Agile community.

Elisabeth's approach to transformation is deeply rooted in her belief that sustainable change begins with people. She has worked extensively with both co-located and globally distributed teams, providing innovative and strategic business solutions that prioritize human connection alongside organizational efficiency. Her contagious enthusiasm and collaborative work ethic have earned her a reputation as a catalyst for positive change in environments ranging from startup ventures to *Fortune* 500 companies.

Known for her ability to bridge communication and leadership gaps, Elisabeth has become a prominent voice in the Agile community, delivering high-caliber thought leadership through coaching, training, and public speaking engagements worldwide. She lives by Aristotle's principle that "we are what we repeatedly do. Excellence, then, is not an act, but a habit," a philosophy that shapes both her professional practice and personal approach to continuous improvement.

When not transforming organizations or speaking at international conferences, Elisabeth enjoys life in the Denver area with her husband and their two beloved dogs. Faith and family form her cornerstone, football fuels her weekends (Broncos or bust!), travel enriches her soul, and gaming remains her carefully guarded secret (until now).

For more information about Elisabeth's work and speaking engagements, visit cornerstoneagility.com or connect with her on LinkedIn.

 /ELISABETHWHITE

Cornerstone Agility Inc. is a values-based, principles-driven transformation, coaching, and training consulting firm built on the cornerstone of excellence.

We're a small group of tight-knit, well-traveled, and well-seasoned leaders who have now led more successful change initiatives than we can count.

Together, we take our clients' transformations beyond theory to design a blueprint for success. Our promise is to maintain integrity through accuracy, honesty, and trustworthiness.

That's our story, and we're sticking to it.